Foraging Mushrooms Identification Field Guide of the Pacific Norhwest:

Book II in the Regional Edible Foraging Series

Armand Hansen

direct or indirect, that are incurred as a result of the use of the information contained within this document, including, but not limited to, errors, omissions, or inaccuracies.

Table of Contents

Your Free Gift!

As a thank you for choosing this book, we've included this handy guide to the hiking trails of the Pacific Northwest, specially written for foragers, as a free gift for our readers.

In this guide, you'll find:

- An overview of the hiking trails of the Pacific Northwest, and which are the best to forage on
- Important information about the plant life and climate of each trail, to ensure you have the best hiking and foraging experience possible

- Essential safety notes, such as which trails pass through bear country, that every hiker or forager should know
- And so much more!

Grab it here: https://armandhansen.com/your-free-gift/

Introduction

Foraging—or the practice of harvesting wild plants for personal consumption—is currently skyrocketing in popularity. If you've picked up this book, you're probably looking to get started foraging for mushrooms in the Pacific Northwest! Whether you're an experienced forager exploring a new area, a beginner looking for a detailed guide to identifying the PNW's edible mushrooms, or simply a mushroom enthusiast, you've come to the right place.

The damp, cool climate of the PNW is ideal for many species of mushrooms, and so foragers flock to the region from far and wide. However, while the landscape of the PNW is one of the most gorgeous on Earth, it can also be treacherous. Since many edible mushroom species have inedible—or even deadly poisonous—lookalikes, it's essential to be *absolutely certain* what species a mushroom is before taking it home. Finally, in order to stay safe foraging for mushrooms in the PNW (or anywhere else), it's important to keep your wits about you and know how to get the job done right.

That's where we come in! In this extensive, beginner-friendly guide, we'll discuss everything you need to know to forage for mushrooms in the beautiful wilderness of British Columbia, Idaho, Washington, and Oregon. We'll talk about what kind of landscape and climate you're facing, and what to do if you come face to face with wildlife. We'll also discuss how to forage ethically, and what to do when you get the mushrooms home. But most importantly, Section 2 of this book will tell you just how to identify the best edible mushrooms of the Pacific Northwest, with high-definition color photos to help you safely distinguish the most delicious specimens from the deadliest.

Foraging is becoming more and more popular as a way to get back to nature, get some exercise, and get healthy food on the table for yourself or your family. If you're a mushroom-lover ready to start harvesting the diverse edible mushrooms of the beautiful Pacific Northwest, read on— this book is for you.

Section 1:

About the Pacific Northwest

The Pacific Northwest is a heavily forested region of northwestern North America, starting from the Pacific coast and extending to the Cascade mountains in the east! All in all, the Pacific Northwest comprises the Canadian province of British Columbia as well as three American states: Washington, Idaho, and Oregon. Some broader definitions include parts of California, Montana, and Alaska, but as most sources follow the definition above, we'll stick to that! Boasting a total area of over 655,000 kilometers, the Pacific Northwest is one of the most breathtaking and biologically diverse regions in the world.

In this section, we'll describe some features of the PNW you need to know about before you start foraging. Some of these features will help you find mushrooms—for example, many mushrooms grow in damp areas or near hardwood trees. Others—such as the presence of dangerous wildlife and sometimes unpredictable weather patterns are included to help you keep yourself safe. Finally, at the end of the chapter we'll give you a list of the national parks in the PNW—so long as you can find a method of transport, you may not have to live on the edge of the woods to get started foraging!

Climate

The climate of the PNW is very nice—most of the time! There are reasons this region is highly favored by hikers, hunters, foragers, and other outdoors-people, and along with its rich biodiversity and beautiful scenery, the climate is one of them. According to meteorologists, the climate of most of the PNW is "temperate oceanic." This refers to climates that are cool in winter and warm in summer, with average temperatures year-round between 32 and 72 degrees Fahrenheit.

Temperate oceanic climates have no dry season, and the amount of precipitation is more or less consistent during all four seasons. There are smaller regions of the Pacific Northwest with other climate types. The climate of the mountainous regions at high elevations is *alpine*, which involves yearly average temperatures under 50 degrees Fahrenheit—but this starts at elevations too high for trees to grow, so you probably won't be foraging there! The climates of regions just east of the mountains can be temperate or hot and dry arid/semi-arid climates, while some of the major cities and surrounding areas have *Mediterranean* climates, characterized by warm, dry summers and high atmospheric pressure.

Overall, the climate of the PNW is not particularly hostile! However, there are a couple things to keep in mind for the sake of preparedness and safety. As we just stated, average temperatures in the PNW are fairly cool compared to the rest of the world, but not below freezing. But don't forget that these are *averages*. During the middle of summer the temperature can get as high as 90 degrees Fahrenheit, and it can also drop well below freezing in winter.

Furthermore, the fall season in the Pacific Northwest is known for being unpredictable. It's possible for a day to start out pleasant, but then take a hard turn into stormy winter weather with little to no warning. If you're planning to go out foraging in the fall, be extra careful by double-checking the forecast, dressing in layers, and letting someone know where you're going.

The Pacific Northwest is the rainiest place in the United States, getting over 7 feet of precipitation on average! But there are much rainier areas than that in the PNW—Some mountainous regions in Washington get 12.5 feet of annual precipitation on average—that's 3.5 feet more than the average yearly rainfall of the Amazon Rainforest! Not all of that precipitation is rain, however—the PNW gets plenty of snow in winter, which falls particularly heavily in mountainous regions.

Landscape

The landscape of the PNW is sparsely populated, with only a few large cities—the most important of them Portland in Oregon, Seattle, Spokane, and Tacoma in Washington, Boise and Meridian in Idaho, and Vancouver, Surrey, and Richmond in British Columbia. Wikipedia lists 41 cities in the Pacific Northwest with populations over 75,000. Dozens of Indigenous Canadian or Native American nations also call the Pacific Northwest home, including but certainly not limited to the Tlingit, Chinook, Sahaptin, and Coast and Interior Salish peoples.

Most of the Pacific Northwest is still covered in wilderness, including forests, wetlands, and quite famously, mountains.

Forests

Two main types of forests exist throughout the Pacific Northwest—temperate rainforests, as well as conifer forests. Both of these are excellent places to forage, and both boast unique ranges of mushroom and fungal species!

The temperate rainforests of the PNW are defined as those with a yearly rainfall of over ten feet and average yearly temperatures between 50 and 75 degrees Fahrenheit. Spend time in these areas and you'll be caught in the rain eventually, but snow is much more unusual! While temperate rainforests are different from coniferous forests, the PNW's temperate rainforests are still heavily populated by conifers, like the coastal sequoia, Douglas fir, spruce, pine, hemlock, and more! However, contrary to the coniferous forests found in the rest of the PNW, the temperate rainforests of the Pacific Northwest usually *also* boast a healthy population of broad-leaved trees, which are also known as hardwoods. Some examples of these are oaks (like the majestic Oregon white oak), red alders, black cottonwoods, and bigleaf maples. What's more, in these areas you'll also find a lush underlayer of green, moisture-loving plants, as well as a rich diversity of symbiotic and parasitic plants, mosses, and fungi that grow *on* the trees themselves. Wildfires are uncommon in temperate rainforests, and rarely spread far.

The temperate rainforests of the Pacific Northwest are mostly found along Western coastal areas. By contrast, the coniferous forests of the PNW are more common in the interior, where summers lean somewhat warmer and dryer though still temperate. One interesting fact about the PNW's coniferous forests is that they were not destroyed in the late Pleistocene period, which was characterized by glacial movements, changes in climate, and mass extinctions. This all occurred between c. 129,000 and c. 11,700 years ago, so these forests have had a long time to become exquisitely suited to their climate and landscape! As a result, trees in coniferous forests in the PNW grow extremely tall and live for extremely long periods.

In these old-growth forests, the massive size of the conifers makes it difficult for broad-leaved hardwoods to grow because they block out most of the sun from above. Furthermore, the climate is such that hardwood trees cannot photosynthesize in most coniferous areas for most of the year. As a result, you'll see far fewer hardwoods in these areas, if at all. Instead, you'll see tall, broadly distributed populations of various subspecies of spruce, fir, pine, hemlock, and larch. The coniferous forests of the Pacific Northwest face wildfires at regular intervals, which are not destructive but essential to the ecology of the region.

There are a number of famous mountain ranges in the Pacific Northwest, including the Cascade Mountains, which extend from the south of British Columbia down the entire coast of the PNW to end in California. Other important ranges include the Coast Mountains down the coast of British Columbia, the Rocky Mountains in the interior of British Columbia, the Klamath Mountains in the southwest of Oregon and the Oregon Coast Range, as well as the Olympic Mountains and the Tatoosh Mountains, both in Washington. Mountainous regions have a "tree line" above which most plants don't grow, but this is relatively high up. It's worth checking out the lower parts of the PNW's breathtaking mountain ranges as a forager, as some mushroom species thrive at higher elevations—and you should make an effort to see these mountains regardless!

The Pacific Northwest also boasts wetlands, which are defined as marshy, swampy areas that are absolutely saturated with water. Washington State is especially famous for its ample wetlands. The wetlands of the PNW are actually essential to the climate of not just the PNW, but the *world*, as they act as *carbon sinks* that soak up millions of tons of carbon dioxide! It's hard to walk through the middle of a swamp—unless you want to end up waist-deep in muddy water or trapped in the mud! However, plenty of mushroom species thrive in the regions *around* Washington's rich wetlands thanks to the cool, damp climate.

Wildlife

The Pacific Northwest is home to a vast range of incredible wild animals, birds, and fish—it's just as much a destination for hunters, recreational fishers, wildlife photographers, and birdwatchers as it is for foragers! Depending on your specific region and the features of the local landscape, you might encounter grizzly bears, brown bears, crested puffins, river otters, sea otters, gray wolves, coyotes, deer, elk, snakes, lizards, skinks, bats, bobcats, cougars, bison, and more!

When you go out foraging, it's important to remember that you are not the only one in the woods. It's important to respect the space and the environment of the animals who live there, for your safety, their safety, and the safety of the environment!

Most animals don't want to harm or eat humans—we aren't the natural prey of any animal in the PNW! However, humans have been encroaching more and more on animal habitats in recent years thanks to logging, new housing developments, tourism, and an increased interest in outdoor activities. Furthermore, animals are now more likely to come across trash cans containing food or to be fed by uninformed tourists, causing them to associate humans with easy sources of food—leading to more confrontations that endanger the safety of both humans and animals.

There are certain rules to follow that can help you keep yourself and the animals of the PNW you safe while you forage. It's important to be aware of your surroundings as you go, keeping an eye (and ear!) out for signs animals are nearby, so you can avoid surprising each other. If you see an animal in the wild, it's alright to view it from a safe distance, but leave it in peace and don't try to interact or get closer. Remember, you're in *their* space, not the other way around.

Similarly, if you find an animal den or nest, even if it seems like the inhabitants aren't present, leave it alone or you could damage it without realizing! The nest's inhabitants might be watching you or able to catch your scent even if you can't see them, and learning that a larger animal has discovered their home would frighten many animals into abandoning it.

Animals, like humans, are fiercely protective of their babies, and one of the most dangerous things you can do is get too close to a wild animal's young, or put yourself between them. An animal that concludes you're a threat to their offspring are vastly more likely to attack, leading to the injury or death of one or both of you. If you see animal young, eggs, or signs of a den or nest, leave them alone, no matter how curious you are!

As the common saying goes, "They're more afraid of you than you are of them." Most animals will flee when they come face to face with a human, but any animal that feels cornered is liable to lash out in self-defense, and some are especially dangerous. These are mostly large carnivores—specifically bears, wolves, and cougars—that are apex predators in the forest and that don't feel automatically threatened by other large animals. Other animals, particularly snakes, are slower moving, equipped with camouflage, and prefer to hide rather than run—but still pack a venomous punch when they defend themselves.

In the subsection below, we'll be giving some basic tips on bear, wolf, cougar, and snake safety in the Pacific Northwest! Keep in mind that this is a general guide. If your local ordinances give different advice, follow the advice of local experts.

Bears

There are two types of bear in the PNW: smaller, shyer black bears, and larger, more aggressive grizzlies/brown bears. While bears can certainly be intimidating, most bears would rather avoid humans and won't attack unless they feel threatened. However, bears venturing onto campgrounds have discovered trash cans, a very convenient source of food for crafty omnivores like themselves. As a result, bear encounters are more likely now than they used to be, as bears regularly return to where the food is!

When in bear country, always make an effort to be visible, and talk as you walk through the woods so that nearby bears aren't surprised by a human's sudden appearance. Identifying yourself as a human by talking will prevent bears from approaching you to see if you're something they can eat, and increase the likelihood they'll move away when they hear you coming! On the flip side, pay attention to your surroundings to reduce the chance a bear will surprise *you*.

If you see a bear cub, you should immediately leave the vicinity, as the mother is almost certainly close by. Bears are *extremely* protective of their young. Never approach, touch, or feed a bear cub, no matter how cute it is!

If you encounter a bear, the most important thing is to *stay calm and not show*. Even though bears can be dangerous, most encounters end without injury to either party. Running away will tell the bear you are food, as will screaming, making other fearful, high-pitched, trembly noises, or making yourself smaller by lowering your posture. These are all understandable reactions, but they're also the reactions the bear's natural prey would have!

Instead, try to act in a way that will convince the bear that you're *not* prey, but that you don't pose any threat. Pick up any small children immediately, and start slowly backing away. Speak in a calm, slow, soft voice. Looking the bear in the eye will be perceived as a threat, so avoid that. If the bear doesn't become more aggressive keep going until you can turn around and *walk* to safety. Don't run when the bear is nearby, or it may instinctively chase you!

So what if you're faced with a bear attack? Bears will generally charge into a fight on all fours, and they move shockingly fast considering their size. Old advice for surviving a bear attack is to climb a tree, but be aware that both grizzly and black bears can climb. If you can make it to a tree and climb it, it could be an option.

Running away, however, is still a bad idea as it will entice the bear to chase you. A charging bear may not be looking to eat you or to fight—it might just be saying, "This is my territory, so don't come any closer!" Continue avoiding eye contact, plant your feet, stand your ground firmly, and keep calmly talking—identifying yourself as a human might cause the bear to turn away (remember, most animals can't see as well as we can).

If the bear keeps charging, now it's time to change strategies. Join hands with others you're with, jump up and down, wave your arms, shout in a deep voice, and make direct eye contact—this says, "I'm big and not afraid of you, so back off." Use the Mace or bear spray you should be carrying as soon as the bear is in range—most animals aren't thinking about prey while (temporarily) blinded and in pain!

There's one more situation where you should act defiant and threatening in a bear's presence—when the bear is hunting you. Encountering a mother bear with cubs or surprising a bear who's eating can lead to a defensive attack, but a bear that is wounded or very hungry may decide to take what it can get and attack as a predator. If a bear is circling or following you, follow the advice in the paragraph above for looking threatening.

If a bear physically attacks you, how to survive depends on the species. Grizzly bears, despite being the larger and more aggressive of the two species, are usually attacking in self-defense. If a grizzly bear attacks you, fall to the ground face-first and lock your fingers behind your neck. While this may seem counter-intuitive, open your legs in a V shape. This position makes it harder for the bear to flip you over and protects your neck, throat, and stomach—vulnerable places that grizzly bears instinctively attack. Usually, a grizzly bear will lose interest in a few seconds to minutes when it thinks it has neutralized the "threat." This is historically the most successful way to survive a grizzly attack.

Black bear attacks are different. Since black bears are smaller, shyer, and less aggressive than their larger brown counterparts, they're more likely to run than to fight when they feel threatened. However, black bears will sometimes—and this is rare—attack humans as prey when they're starving or wounded. Therefore, if you're being attacked by a black bear, pretending to be dead won't encourage it to stop since that's what it wants! If you can get into a car or building, do so. If not, fight back with anything you can, including your fists if you have to. Using a stick, rocks, your bag, your fist, or anything else you have on you, show the bear that attacking you is more trouble than it's worth. Chances are good it will give up if you put up enough of a fight!

Wolves

Wolves hunt in packs, and are very stealthy—meaning they can appear very suddenly if you don't know how to identify the signs of their presence. Luckily, most wolves naturally fear humans and will run away at their approach. Unfortunately, for the reasons we talked about above, many wolves are becoming more and more confident with regards to approaching human areas.

Most of the rules around bear safety also apply to wolf safety—talk as you walk through the woods to give nearby animals some warning you're present so they have a chance to move. As with all animals, don't approach wolves if you see them, and *especially* don't approach their cubs!

One thing to note with wolf safety is that if you see a recent carcass of a deer, elk, moose, or other prey animal, don't approach or investigate it. Like humans, wolves don't typically eat a big meal at one sitting! Instead, a pack of wolves who take down a large animal will return to it multiple times over a period of a few days. The pack is likely to still be nearby, may pick up your scent, and will defend their food if they think you're going to take it.

Most encounters with wolves look something like this: A single wolf briefly appears to check out an unfamiliar smell or noise, realizes a human was behind it, and promptly runs away without further incident. But if you meet a wolf or wolves that are acting aggressive (lowered bodies, pinned-back ears, direct eye contact, bared teeth, growling, salivating), that don't seem to be afraid of you, if there's more than one, or if they appear to be stalking you, the situation gets much more serious.

Unlike bears, with wolves you should indicate you're not going to be an easy target as soon as you know they're following you. The Parks of British Columbia official website recommends never letting a wolf get closer to you than 100 meters, and states you should start trying to scare an approaching wolf off *well* before that. As with bears, pick up small children as soon as you notice the wolves to stop them from running or shrieking. Open your jacket, wave your arms or a stick, lift your bag over your head, yell in a deep voice, throw rocks, and/or use an air horn or whistle to make a loud noise. All of these tactics will make you seem big and scary, increasing the odds a wolf or wolf pack will decide you're too dangerous to attack.

If an aggressive wolf is approaching you, don't look the animal in the eye and back away slowly while continuing to be loud and scary. Watch your step—tripping and falling down will trigger the wolf's instinct to pounce! Be aware that a lone wolf is probably not actually alone, and keep your eyes and ears peeled for more in the surrounding area. If the wolf lets you go—which is the most likely result if you follow these steps—back away until you can walk, not run, to safety.

If the wolf or pack attacks, especially if you're alone, things are not looking good. Your best chance is to curl into a ball and cover vulnerable areas as well as you can. Wolves prefer to attack the face, throat, ribs, stomach, and neck, and also prefer to take down fleeing prey, so this discourages them. Fighting back is recommended by some guides, but in an interview with Insider magazine wolf expert Oliver Starr mentions that he has actually *been* attacked by a wolf before and states from experience that this would not be a winnable fight for most people. Instead, he recommends the "ball" strategy (Spector, 2012).

Last of all, bear spray is not just for bears! The irritants it contains is a perfectly workable self-defense weapon against wolves, so if you're being stalked or attacked by wolves, use it when they come in range.

Mountain Lions

Also known as cougars and pumas, mountain lions are large feline predators that primarily hunt deer and similar hoofed prey animals, but will also happily feed on unlucky small game that wander past their dens. They are primarily active at dusk, dawn, and night, and hunt by stealthily stalking their prey and pouncing on their backs, knocking them to the ground and immediately delivering a swift killing bite to the skull, back of the neck, or spine. They commonly lie in wait on top of elevated places like boulders or ledges, which are plentiful in their mountain habitat.

If you can avoid it, don't go into rocky, hilly, or mountainous areas in the evening, the early morning, or at night, as lower levels of light make it easier for a hungry mountain lion to camouflage—and they're more active during these low-light conditions. Be aware of your surroundings—are there a lot of rocky outcrops, hills, cliffs, or banks you need to walk close to? Can you easily see what's behind and above you?

Foraging with at least one other adult will make mountain lions much less likely to attack—as you can see from their hunting strategy, they're great at taking down one animal, but will be discouraged if they think it would make them vulnerable to attack. If you have children with you, keep them close to your side in mountain lion country—they're more attractive prey than you are!

If a mountain lion pounces on you from behind, protect your head and the back of your neck, yell for help, and try to fight back as well as you can. Some guides suggest trying to stay on your feet, but since mountain lions can get up to 200 pounds in weight, this may not be possible. While this scenario seldom *actually* occurs, it's a great example of why foraging in groups is safer than foraging alone!

What happens if you come face to face with a mountain lion? If you're facing each other, you've already thrown off their natural hunting strategy, but that doesn't mean you're safe. Don't run because this will cause the mountain lion to instinctively chase you. Remain calm and pick up children, but avoid bending down, crouching, or lowering your head when you do this. Mountain lions instinctively pounce on exposed necks and backs, especially when they're horizontal, like a deer or mountain goat's.

As with wolves, if you've been approached by a mountain lion, don't wait to start acting aggressive. Use the tips above or whatever you can think of to make yourself look bigger and more threatening. Without looking the cat in the eye, back away slowly until you can safely leave the area. Make sure that the mountain lion has a way to leave the situation that doesn't require it to move toward you—if it doesn't have this, it might not realize you aren't trying to corner it.

Rarely, these steps won't work, and the mountain lion will still attack. A mountain lion that lowers its body, bares its teeth, pins back its ears and makes direct eye contact is threatening to pounce. Don't assume it's too far away to do that—mountain lions can leap distances of up to 40 feet.

If you see this, *continue backing away without running*, throw rocks or objects at the mountain lion, and keep yelling and making yourself big. You want to show it that you're too dangerous to attack. If the mountain lion attacks, fight back by whatever means necessary. If you have bear spray, use it! Otherwise, use your fists and/or whatever items you have on hand to defend yourself. You don't have to take the cat down—remember, they'll probably give up if attacking you isn't worth it.

Venomous Snakes

In our last section on how to deal with dangerous animal encounters, we're going to pivot to an entirely different kind of creature! Most people don't think of the Pacific Northwest when they think of venomous snakes, they do exist in the area—*one* species specifically, the Western rattlesnake (*Crotalus oreganus*). While other species that are technically venomous can be found throughout the area, only the Western rattlesnake's venom packs enough of a punch to be dangerous to humans. Getting bitten by a Western rattlesnake is a medical emergency, but nowadays bites are rare, and deaths even rarer.

The first step of venomous safety is to be appropriately dressed—wear thick, closed toe boots and long pants tucked in (see Section 3 for more reasons this is appropriate clothing for foraging).

A fully-grown Western rattlesnake is between two and five feet long. In order to camouflage in the diverse forests of the Pacific Northwest, these snakes can be found in a range of colors that vary according to where they're found. The body of Western rattlesnakes may be light to dark brown, greenish, reddish, grayish, or yellowish-brown, tan, or olive. Despite the variance in color, the main identifying feature of the species is the oval-shaped blotches that evenly pattern the back and sides of the snake, which are surrounded by a light beige or cream rim or halo. As the snake's body narrows toward the tail and rattle, these dark blotches turn into bands. The head is triangular and attached to the body by a slim, distinct neck.

Western rattlesnakes make their communal dens on the sides of hills, but also rely on mice, rats, voles, and other small rodents as their main source of food—and these are most abundant in forests with rocky ground, where adult snakes migrate for the summer, with one exception— pregnant snakes remain close to the den during this period until they lay their eggs in fall.

Western rattlesnakes hunt by laying very still until their prey wanders within range, and then ambush them with a deadly venomous bite. How do they avoid getting stepped on by large animals? These snakes rattle in response to the vibrations and heat waves animals (like us) give off as they walk over the ground. This is the snake's way of saying "I'm here, and I'm venomous, so don't come any closer!"

Learning to recognize the sound of the Western rattlesnake's rattle is essential to safe foraging in the PNW. It doesn't sound like a baby's rattle, but more like a "buzz." We suggest looking up the sound on YouTube to familiarize yourself before heading out! If you hear that sound, stop walking and work out where it's coming from, then give it a wide berth. Be sure to give the snake space to move away from you, as they're more likely to attack when they feel cornered or threatened.

As you're walking through the woods, pay attention to where you're stepping. Western rattlesnakes will hide under brush, bushes, leaves, and rocks, as well as inside crevices, under uprooted trees, behind fallen logs, and so on. They may also lay on or between rocks warmed by the sun to warm themselves up. Avoid stepping on, turning over, or moving rocks unless absolutely necessary.

Snakes rest in underbrush, piles of leaves, and tall grass during the day before hunting in lower-light conditions, so be especially wary of these spots during daylight hours. If the snake is hidden behind a large stump, rock, or fallen tree, it may not be expecting you because of the way its sensory organs work—by registering heat. If you encounter this kind of obstacle, walk around it instead of over it, or step on top of it and check where your foot is going to land before descending on the other side.

What should you do if you *do* get bitten by a Western rattlesnake while foraging? Don't panic—as long as you get medical attention ASAP, you'll most likely be okay!

Be aware that symptoms of rattlesnake venom poisoning include swelling and discoloration around the bite, numbness and tingling in the face, extremities and limbs, blurry vision, dizziness, nausea and vomiting, feeling weak or faint, and sweating and/or salivating excessively. Familiarizing yourself with these symptoms can help you stay calm if the worst happens because you won't be wondering if what you're feeling is normal.

If you get bitten by a Western rattlesnake, the foraging trip is over! You need to get away from the snake at once, as they will attack again if one bite doesn't make that happen. Leave the woods, use your cell phone to call 911 as soon as you can, and listen to all operators' instructions. Remember what the snake looked like or snap a photo with your phone if possible, as this will help medical professionals confirm the species and start the correct treatment as fast as possible.

Rattlesnake venom circulates through your blood, damaging the cells of the organs and tissues it reaches. Therefore, while you make your way to the emergency room, you need to slow your circulation as much as possible. Avoid strenuous exercise, and only walk if necessary. If someone is not with you who can drive you to the hospital, call an ambulance and then follow the dispatcher's instructions with regards to staying put and finding the responders. Don't put pressure on the bite or try to stop the bleeding—just cover it with a sterile bandage if you have one. Bleeding can help wash some lingering venom out of the wound, and cutting off circulation to the affected limb will increase damage. Hold the affected limb **below** your chest.

If you feel disoriented, shivery, and thirsty, you may be dealing with shock. This means the situation is more serious. If this happens, lay down with your feet elevated, sip water if you can, try to keep warm, and wait for help to arrive. This is one reason why it's a good idea to have some way to signal distress, like a flare, when you go out of cell service range—or better yet, someone with you!

There's a lot of outdated bad advice about dealing with rattlesnake bites out there. **Here are some things you should absolutely <u>not</u> do:**

- Apply a tourniquet or otherwise cut off circulation to the limb.
- Squeeze, bite, suck, cut, press, or otherwise mess with the bite.
- Wash the bite with water.
- Apply ice.
- Move around *any* more than necessary to get to safety.
- Try to catch the rattlesnake and bring it with you.

Finding a Place to Forage in the PNW

Where are you going to go to forage, if you're not one of the lucky few with forested land they own? If you don't know someone who will let you forage on *their* land, you might have to take a hike! In this section, we're going to give you a quick list of the main national parks to look into—if we included all provincial parks and hiking trails, they'd need a book of their own. Be aware that rules with regards to foraging vary depending on the location, and you should always respect local laws and regulations first and foremost. Each of these parks has at least a handful of hiking trails that will take you through the full range of the PNW's scenic beauty, and afford plenty of mushroom hunting opportunities!

Pacific Northwest National Parks

British Columbia

- Pacific Rim National Park Reserve
- Gulf Islands National Park Reserve
- Mount Revelstoke National Park
- Kootenay National Park
- Glacier National Park
- Yoho National Park
- Gwaii Haanas National Park

Washington

- Olympic National Park
- Mount Rainier National Park
- Mount St. Helens National Park

Oregon

- Crater Lake National Park
- Oregon National Historic Trail
- Lewis and Clark National Historic Trail

Idaho

- Yellowstone National Park
- City of Rocks National Reserve

Edible Mushrooms of the

Pacific Northwest

The moment you've been waiting for is here—in this section, we'll look at 25 key edible mushroom species you'll be able to find throughout the Pacific Northwest, if you know where to look! While we chose species from lists of edible mushrooms rated as easy to identify, we'll also note whether each mushroom species has any inedible lookalikes, and how to tell them apart. Remember: Never eat a mushroom if you have even the *slightest* doubt about what it is!

Parts of the Mushroom

Before we get into profiling the edible mushroom species of the PNW, there's a little terminology to get out of the way. If you're an experienced mushroom forager, you might choose to skip this section, but if you're new to mushroom foraging, you don't want to miss this!

Fruit/Fruiting Body

The fruit, or fruiting body, of a mushroom is the part you pick—in other words, the entirety of what you see above ground. Fruiting bodies can be umbrella-shaped, funnel-shaped, disk-shaped, and more—mushrooms and fungi are just as diverse as animals and plants!

Mycelium

While you can't see the mycelium, it's much, *much* larger than the mushroom cap—and it's all underground. Many people view mycelium as the "roots" of the mushroom, but it's much more fascinating than that. This network of living fibers allows mushrooms to feed on decaying matter in the soil, but it also connects mushrooms in different locations in vast networks. If a mushroom is picked correctly, and conditions stay favorable, then the mycelium allows the mushroom to grow back. If conditions are poor—for example, if there's an extended drought or little to no nutrients available—the mycelium can become dormant for years and start to fruit again once things turn around!

Cap

As the name may suggest, the *cap* is the "hat" that sits on top of the mushroom's stem, with gills on its underside. Mushroom caps vary wildly in color, size, shape, and texture.

Gills

Peeling back the cap of a mushroom, you'll notice rows of thin structures on the underside. A mushroom's gills are there to produce and release *spores*, which are the microscopic "seeds" that allow new mycelium and new mushrooms to grow. Like caps, gills vary wildly in size, shape, and color. Some species have ridges, pores, or needles instead of gills, which serve the same purpose.

Stem/Stipe

The stem of the mushroom is exactly what you'd assume! Also called the stipe, a mushroom's stem helps it spread its spores by lifting the cap and gills high enough off the ground that the spores can disperse. Some mushrooms don't have stems at all, and instead disperse their spores through different mechanisms.

Volva

While not all mushrooms have volvas, they are a distinctive feature of the species that do. The volva is a "universal veil" that protects juvenile mushrooms as they grow, which naturally breaks when they get too big for it. On a mature mushroom, the volva appears as a bulb-like shape at the base of the stem.

Skirt

Not all mushrooms have a skirt, so it can be a useful way to tell one species from another. An immature mushroom's volva is called a "universal veil" before it breaks, but other species have "partial veils": a thin layer of tissue that covers only the gills of an immature mushroom as it grows. As with the universal veil, it breaks when the mushroom gets big enough that it doesn't need it anymore, leaving a ring of tissue around the middle of the stem. Since this tissue is only attached at one end, it takes on the "fluttering" look of a fashionable skirt!

Spore Print

Above, we mentioned that mushroom spores are microscopic, but remember that mushrooms produce a *lot* of them! Many mushrooms have "spore prints" which refer to powdery dustings of spores around the stem, skirt, and/or volva of a mushroom, from spores falling out of the gills under the caps. The color of the spore print is a key way to tell different mushroom species apart.

Mushroom Seasons

While we include some notes about when to look for each mushroom in the species profile below, we decided to include a handy guide to which mushrooms are in season during which parts of the year in a tabular format! Check it out below.

	Season	Notes
Pacific Golden Chanterelle	July to December	
Black Chanterelle	June to December	Blooms after rainfall
Cauliflower Mushroom	Late summer through fall	
Black Morel	Early spring	Very brief season
King Bolete	Late spring	Season is extended the higher the ground elevation—in mountainous regions can be found throughout summer and even fall
Chicken of the Woods	Spring, summer, and fall	
Oyster Mushroom	Fall	Mild temperatures

	Season	Notes
		and rain extends the season; in British Columbia, start looking for these in spring
Yellow Gilled Russula	Summer into early fall	Bloom after warm weather
Glistening Ink Cap	Spring and fall	Blooms after mild temperature and rainy weather
Horse Mushroom	June-December	Season may start earlier if temperatures are warm
Western Giant Puffball	Late summer through fall	Only safe to eat when young—harvest early in the season
Common Puffball	Fall and winter	Blooms after rain in cool temperatures; if the conditions

	Season	Notes
		are right, the season may start earlier
Slimy Spike Cap	Fall and winter	May be found in spring in some isolated regions
Western Saffron Milk Cap	Early spring through late fall	Blooms approximately 2 days after heavy rain
Meadow Mushroom	Spring, summer, and fall	
Red Cracked Bolete	Spring, summer, and fall	
Jelly Ear Mushroom	Fall and winter	Blooms after cold, wet weather
Hedgehog Mushroom	Summer and fall	
Apricot Jelly Mushroom	Summer and fall	

	Season	Notes
Lion's Mane Mushroom	Late summer and fall	
Fairy Ring Mushroom	Spring into late fall or early winter	Blooms after cool, damp, weather or rain
Comb Toothed Fungus	Late summer to late fall	Warm weather can extend the season
Yellow Swamp Russula	Summer to fall	
Shaggy Mane Mushroom	Late summer to fall	

Mushroom Species Profiles

Pacific Golden Chanterelle (Cantharellus formosus)

Chanterelles are some of the most delicious and highly sought-after mushrooms in the Pacific Northwest and around the world! The Pacific golden chanterelle is native to the PNW, and absolutely abundant in the region. It's also the official state mushroom of the state of Oregon!

Physical Description

As the name suggests, the Pacific golden chanterelle is most distinctive for its bright, rich coloring, which ranges from bright yellow or orange to rich gold. The fruiting body is between ¾ and 5 ½ inches in width. Like other chanterelles, it has a distinctive funnel shape. The cap is smooth on top, while the underside is lined with ridges instead of gills.

While a stereotypical mushroom has a distinct, separate cap and stipe, the Pacific golden chanterelle has a seamless, cohesive body. Instead of being attached only to the cap, the ridges run uninterrupted down the length of the mushroom until they fade into the lower part of the stipe. The ridges may have a pink, salmon, or beige tint, but this isn't present in all specimens. At the top of the mushroom close to the rim of the cap, the ridges start to fork and branch out.

Besides the ridges, the stipe is usually the same color as the cap or slightly paler. The spore print is pale yellow-white.

Where and When to Harvest

The Pacific Golden Chanterelle is in season from July to December, and grows in any and all of the PNW's abundant conifer forests! It is present in all four regions of the PNW but is especially common in Washington and Oregon. It may be found growing alone or in clusters, and in a range of light conditions. Darker, duller specimens are found when the weather has been dry, while wet weather will cause the mushrooms to take on a much more vibrant color.

Pacific golden chanterelles growing in dim conditions, like thickets or heavy shade, will take on a more vibrant pink tinge than those growing in bright sunlight, and may even appear with a mostly-pink cap in very dark conditions.

Uses

The Pacific golden chanterelle is considered one of the most delicious mushrooms of the PNW for its sweet taste, which has been described as floral or fruity. It can be added to virtually any dish where mushrooms are used, and is particularly tasty sauteed in butter.

Warnings and Lookalikes

It's possible for a range of yellow, orange, gold, and tan mushroom species to take on a similar appearance to a Pacific golden chanterelle if their caps are damaged. This can cause them to wrinkle and turn upwards, giving them a false funnel shape. The easiest ways to tell the difference are:

- A Pacific golden chanterelle will smell like fruit. The scent is especially similar to apricots.
- A Pacific golden chanterelle has blunt, forked ridges, not flexible gills. If it has flexible gills, it's not a chanterelle!
- Groups of orange-yellow mushrooms growing with their stems fused at the base are possibly the poisonous *Omphalotus olivascens*, or jack-o'-lantern mushrooms. Pacific golden chanterelles *never* grow this way.
- The poisonous brown roll-rim (*Paxillus involutus*) has a duller, browner cap, flexible gills, and a brown spore print.

Black Chanterelle (Craterellus fallax)

The beautiful black chanterelle has a range of ominous-sounding alternative names, including *trompete de la mort,* or trumpet of the dead, in French! On the flip side, a happier common name for this species is *horn of plenty.*

Physical Description

Fruiting bodies of black chanterelles are approximately 3 inches in diameter, give or take. The most striking aspect of this distinctive mushroom is its color. Up close, the cap of the black chanterelle is dark brown, dark gray, or black. Some specimens have a purplish tint. The outside of the cap and the stem usually take a dark gray color.

Like other chanterelles, the black chanterelle has a distinctive funnel/trumpet shape. In older specimens, the rim of the cap will flare out and become wrinkled and frayed. On the underside of the cap, there are no ridges or gills. One distinct feature of this mushroom is that the cap and upper part of the stem are hollow, hence the comparison to the Thanksgiving cornucopia. The flesh of the cap is thin, but hard to break.

Where and When to Harvest

While black chanterelles and related species grow around the world, in the PNW, they are in season from June to December. They grow better during wet periods, and will take on a richer black color in conditions with plenty of moisture.

Look for black chanterelles growing at the base of broad-leaved trees like oaks and beeches, especially in moist patches of moss or rotting plant matter. These damp, dim, fecund environments are just what this species needs to grow. You may need to actually approach these tree species and examine the ground around their roots for black chanterelles—since they camouflage with the dark ground, they're usually not visible when you just pass by!

Black chanterelles grow in clusters, joined at the base: They have been described as looking like bouquets of flowers! If you find a patch of black chanterelles, look closely at the ground in the area around it: There are likely to be more! If you see patches of true chanterelles like the Pacific golden chanterelle, this is another sign that black chanterelles are close by.

The black chanterelle has a pleasant taste that has been compared to butter and wood smoke. However, they need to be cooked for at least 10 minutes, usually more, before they are edible due to their tough texture. Thanks to their striking appearance, they are sometimes roasted and served at room temperature on charcuterie boards with cured meats, olives, and cheeses, which complement their savory flavor. They also pair well with fish dishes, and produce a black liquid run-off during cooking that can be used as a sauce for a fish entree.

If you're interested in drying mushrooms to preserve them, don't overlook this species. Thanks to their tough flesh, black chanterelles can be dried and reconstituted without losing much of their flavor.

Warnings and Lookalikes

Thanks to their distinctive appearance, black chanterelles have few lookalikes, and no poisonous look-alikes in the PNW. If you ensure the mushroom you found has *all* of the traits described above, it's definitely a black chanterelle.

Cauliflower Mushroom (Sparassis crispa)

Is that a cauliflower growing on the forest floor? No—it's a cauliflower mushroom, one of the strangest looking and most unusual fungi in the PNW!

Physical Description

As the name suggests, the cauliflower mushroom looks just like a head of cauliflower. The mushroom is always white, off-white, or white tinged with yellow or brown. The inner flesh has a firm texture. The outside of the mushroom should feel a little spongy and take on a wavy "rosette" appearance. The "leaves" of the rosette are not one unified mushroom cap, but grow from a group of conjoined branches that are hidden inside the fungus.

The cauliflower mushroom's fruiting body can reach almost a foot in diameter. It lacks a visible stem, pores, gills, or other features characteristic of other mushrooms.

Where and When to Harvest

The cauliflower mushroom comes into season in later summer, and can be found throughout the fall. Look for the cauliflower mushroom in conifer forests, at or near the bases of large trees or stumps. You may find one alone, or a small group.

Uses

The cauliflower mushroom has a mild, pleasant mushroom-y flavor. It's tough enough to be breaded, deep fried, and used as an alternative to chicken nuggets!

Since cut-up cauliflower mushroom florets take a "noodly" texture when cooked, they can also be used as a much lower-carb substitute for noodles! They are also a popular addition to pasta dishes, or even used as a low-carb pasta alternative!

Cauliflower mushroom florets can also be sauteed in butter with herbs like rosemary and oregano to make a tasty side that pairs well with red meat and pork.

Beware that cauliflower mushrooms hold a lot of water, so cook them slowly in order to give this a chance to evaporate or you could end up with an unpleasant, watery dish!

The cauliflower mushroom is so unusual-looking, you don't really have to worry about picking up a poisonous lookalike, as long as the specimen you've found has all of the traits above. The only lookalike that is similar enough in appearance is a closely related edible species, *Sparassis spathulata*, which is almost identical except that each fruiting body has multiple stems or stalks instead of one stalk with multiple branches.

Black Morel (Morchella elata)

The striking black morel might not be the most attractive mushroom in the PNW, but this highly coveted prize is definitely one of the tastiest!

Physical Description

The most distinctive physical characteristic of the black morel, like all edible true morels, is hollow on the inside. If you find a mushroom that *looks* like a morel but is not hollow, it is *not* a black morel but an inedible lookalike.

The *second* most distinctive characteristic of the black morel is the cap! Black morel caps are about 8 cm/3 inches in length and pointed at the top (almost like a beehive, but more elongated). It has a characteristic "honeycomb" shape covered in pits! The color of the cap is dark brown, brown-black or black, and gets darker as the mushroom matures. The cap does not have a gilled or porous underside—the base of the cap is attached directly to the stem and *never* hangs loose.

The stem of the morel is white, off-white, or grayish-white, and has a bulbous volva at the base. It is also hollow and has a smooth exterior. The stem should not be of regular shape or symmetrical—usually it's at least a little curved or crooked.

Where and When to Harvest

The black morel has a brief season in early spring. You can find it in conifer forests, at or near the bases of conifers, where it may be alone or in a group scattered over a patch. If you know of a conifer forest that has been logged or that has been affected by a wildfire, check for black morels in these areas the next spring, as these create perfect conditions for black morels to grow.

Uses

The delicious flavor and tender texture of the black morel make it a perfect addition to soups, stews, and pasta sauces. It can also be sliced up, sauteed, and added to Asian-inspired noodle soups as a garnish. But the most unique use of the black morel is that it's perfect for stuffing—try making your favorite stuffed bell pepper recipe with black morels next time!

The flavor of morels is delicious, but mild, so if you're looking to pair it with meat, cheeses, or wine, it goes well with most things! Hermitage Blanc is a light white wine that pairs especially well with black morel dishes.

Warnings and Lookalikes

There are a number of very similar morel species in the PNW that come in season at different times. We chose to highlight the black morel as it is easiest to identify for its striking black color. However, *all* true morels are edible, and depending on the subspecies can be grayish, tan, brown, bluish, or yellow. If a specimen you find has these traits, it is definitely a morel:

- The honeycomb cap is attached at the underside, and does not hang loose in an umbrella shape like other mushrooms.
- The entire fruiting body—stem and cap—are hollow. If it's not hollow, it's not a morel.

The false morels in the PNW are inedible or even poisonous, so as always it's *essential* to be absolutely sure!

It's possible, but not proven or disproven, that morels can become toxic when they interact with alcohol. Just in case, it's best to avoid alcohol while enjoying these delicious fungi.

King Bolete (Boletus edulis)

If this oversized royal mushroom looks familiar, it might be because it's one of the most highly sought-after wild mushrooms in the world! The king bolete is also known as the pink porcini for its cheerful color.

Physical Description

The king bolete is a large mushroom—the cap alone can have a diameter of up to a foot! The cap of the highly coveted king bolete can be yellow-brown, red-brown, deep rust-red, plain brown, and tan. The cap may or may not feel sticky to the touch. Some foragers describe the cap as looking like a toasted hamburger bun (The Greedy Vegan, 2015)!

On the underside of the cap, you'll find pores instead of gills—the surface should be very porous and resemble a sponge. The underside if white, or off-white in young specimens and turns gray-brown, dull yellowish-brown, olive, or plain brown as the mushroom grows.

Like the cap, the stem of the king bolete is large and thick, taking a white, off-white, or brown hue. There is a visible bulb, or volva, at the base of the stem in younger specimens.

When you cut open a possible king bolete specimen, the flesh should remain white and not bruise blue, red, or any other color.

Where and When to Harvest

The king bolete is in season in late spring throughout the PNW, but if you live in a region with higher elevation, it can be found through the summer and occasionally even into the fall. In other words, the higher the elevation, the longer the season! This mushroom grows in the soil at the bases of trees, around the roots.

King boletes are often concealed by falling leaves, twigs, and debris, so watch your step as you explore the woods! A little "mound" formed by fallen leaves or other debris is worth cautiously investigating, but be sure to keep our snake safety tips from the previous chapter in mind when doing this.

Uses

The king bolete is described as having a nutty taste—and so, it pairs well with many of the same things nuts do! Like other porcini-type mushrooms, its flavor can be enhanced with savory herbs like oregano, rosemary and thyme. A spritz of lemon juice can serve to brighten up a dish centering this delicious fungi!

In Italian cuisine, porcini mushrooms, including the king bolete/pink porcini, are often included in risottos. It also pairs well with French red wines like Cabernet Franc and Syrah.

Warnings and Lookalikes

The pores under the cap of the king bolete should be removed before cooking or preserving, as they can absorb basically anything—including things you don't want in your body.

The only major inedible lookalike to the king bolete is a mushroom called *Typholis bellus,* which is also known as the almost-king or the bitter bolete! As both names suggest, foragers are often disappointed when they find an almost-king instead of the delicious porcini they were searching for. Here's how to tell them apart:

- The pores of the almost-king have a pink tinge, whereas the pores of the king bolete are never this color or anything close to it.
- The almost-king has brown "netting" or webbing over the stem.
- Some foragers do a "nibble test" which is exactly as it sounds like. Tasting a pinch-sized piece of almost-king and then spitting it out won't get you sick, but you *will* quickly determine if the flavor is "pleasant and nutty" or "extremely bitter!"
    - However, **we don't recommend doing this test. There's no need to put anything in your mouth to tell these two mushrooms apart, especially when one of the options is an inedible wild plant.**

The chicken of the woods mushroom is named so because young specimens have a texture reminiscent of a perfectly-cooked chicken breast!

Physical Description

The chicken of the woods has no stem, and a shelf or disk-like appearance. The fruiting body is bright "sulfur" yellow or bright orange, and may grow more orange toward the tips. Look for overlapping layers of these growing on moist wood. You may also notice a savory odor from the fruiting body, but you'll have to draw close to smell it as it is very mild.

Most fruiting bodies are around 20 cm in diameter, and have a rubber-like texture that gets soft and pliable around the edges. If you break open a specimen, the flesh on the inside should be white or pale yellow, and have a firm texture like a cooked chicken breast, which again is more pliable around the edges. The soft edges are rippled and wavy in appearance.

On the underside of the disk-like fruiting body, chicken of the woods disperses its spores through a layer of small pores. If you find a specimen with gills or ridges, it's not chicken of the woods! The underside of the body is white or vibrant yellow.

Where and When to Harvest

In the Pacific Northwest, chicken of the woods is in season year-round except for winter. Look for these mushrooms growing on moist, exposed wood. They may be growing on rotting logs on the ground, on gashes or other wounds on trees, or on top of tree stumps—anywhere wood is damp and exposed.

Uses

Chicken of the woods is an extremely nutritious mushroom with plenty of fiber, protein, Vitamin C, and potassium.

The fungus is often fried or sauteed and served with sauce—the porous surface will absorb oils, seasonings, and condiments easily. Because of its texture and relatively high protein content, it can be used as a substitute for meat. Since it has a mild flavor and absorbs sauces well, it can also be used as a substitute for tofu: Simply press with paper towels to remove some moisture before adding pieces to stir-fries or other Asian-inspired dishes. Chicken of the woods can also be breaded, deep fried, and served with plum sauce, barbecue sauce, or anything else you'd dip a deep-fried finger food into!

Warnings and Lookalikes

There are circumstances where chicken of the woods can become inedible:

- Older specimens are pale, brittle, and have a chalk-like texture. These are not edible. If you're unsure, try boiling a piece for 15 minutes, and then see if it's tender at the end. If not, it's too old.
    - Want to avoid accidentally harvesting old chicken of the woods? Simply cut away the soft outsides of a larger specimen—this is the new or younger part of the mushroom!
- Chicken of the woods grows on trees, so if there's anything wrong with the tree it affects the

mushrooms as well. Toxins and other compounds from wood can be inedible or cause allergic reactions in some individuals. Chicken of the woods will last for a week in a paper bag in the fridge, so cook and eat a small portion and then wait a day or two to see if you have a reaction before digging in.

There are two major inedible lookalikes to chicken of the woods, neither of which is deadly:

- The cinnabar polypore (*Pycnoporus cinnabarinus*) has a similar rigid texture to cork, and is not pliable like chicken of the woods. Both the top and the underside have a reddish orange color.

- The tender nesting polypore (*Hapalopilus nidulans*) can grow solitarily *or* in clusters, unlike chicken of the woods which appears in layered clusters. It is cinnamon orange-brown on both sides of the body.

Oyster Mushroom (*Pleurotus ostreatus*)

The oyster mushroom gets its name not from its taste, but its appearance and the clustered way it sometimes grows—just like oysters!

Physical Description

The fruiting bodies of the oyster mushroom are generally at least 9 cm across on the cap, and *can* grow much larger. The cap is off-white, gray, or tan, and is usually described as being asymmetrically shaped like a fan or oyster. In older specimens, the edges of the caps can become frilly or wavy and turn upwards, while in younger specimens, the cap can take on a dome or umbrella-like shape with the edges turned downwards. When growing in large, close clusters, the caps of young oyster mushrooms sometimes turn upwards into a trumpet shape.

One of the most distinctive features of the oyster mushroom is the gills, which are large and extend from the rim of the cap down to the base of the stem. The gills are not frilled or serrated at the edges. The stem and gills are both off-white in most cases. The stem is short and stubby, and may even be completely absent or mostly hidden by the gills.

While the oyster mushroom may not always have a visible spore print, the spore print is pale and variable in color when present.

One last way to identify oyster mushrooms is that they smell good—somewhat like licorice! If you find a foul-smelling specimen, it's either not an oyster mushroom, or there's something wrong with it. Either way, best to leave it alone.

Where and When to Harvest

Oyster mushrooms are primarily in season in the fall, but depending on your local climate they may be found year-round. Foragers in British Columbia especially should keep an eye out for oyster mushrooms in the spring. Oyster mushrooms grow best in mild temperatures and plenty of rain.

Oyster mushrooms are found primarily in the PNW's temperate rainforests, where they grow on the wood of (primarily) hardwood trees like oak, maple, ash, and alder. Since these mushrooms need lots of moisture to thrive, look for them in lush, damp areas, especially near rivers, lakes, and ponds. If you only live near a conifer forest, it's still worth checking for oyster mushrooms—while hardwood trees are preferred, they can and do grow on conifers when no hardwoods are present!

Uses

Oyster mushrooms grow all over the world, where they are a part of many world cuisines, especially in Asia. The mushrooms also became part of German cuisine when people foraged them during WW1, as food was scarce. The mushrooms are lauded for a mild, savory flavor that is described as *umami* in Japanese cuisine.

Oyster mushrooms are almost always eaten cooked to improve their taste and texture, and are a great addition to Asian-inspired stir-fries and noodle dishes. Since they are also relatively large and thick, they are sometimes used as a meat substitute.

Oyster mushrooms can also be dried and reconstituted without losing much of their flavor. Some guides even recommend *not* reconstituting oyster mushrooms before cooking with them, as the mushrooms are so absorbent! Instead, the recommendation is to add pieces of dried mushrooms into a dish, which will then soak up all the sauce and oil around them to become exquisitely flavored.

Warnings and Lookalikes

While it's easy enough to identify oyster mushrooms, look-alikes do exist and it's important to be mindful of them.

- The poisonous velvet-footed pax (*Tapinella atrotomentosa*) has a similar appearance, but grows primarily on conifers. The easiest way to tell them apart is that the velvet-footed pax have longer, thicker stems, the bases of which are covered in a distinctive brownish fuzz. The gills of this lookalike are also separable from the rest of the stem, instead of running down to the base.
- There are numerous inedible lookalikes to the oyster mushroom that have different gill patterns— wavy, serrated, or frilled. A mushroom with any of these features is not an oyster mushroom.
- Avoid specimens that are under 9 cm or approximately 3.5 inches in diameter—this will eliminate smaller lookalike species that may or may not be edible.

Yellow-Gilled Russula (Russula lutea)

The huge *russula* genus of mushrooms, which comprises hundreds of species, tend to resemble how mushrooms appear in cartoons, with thick, round, brightly colored caps!

Physical Description

The cap of the yellow-gilled russula is just under 3 inches in diameter, or around 7 cm in most specimens. It has a convex, mildly umbrella-shaped appearance in younger specimens, and is flatter or depressed in the center in older specimens. Older specimens may also have thin "furrow-lines" (Northern Bushcraft, 2021) around the edges of the cap, somewhat like the thin, parallel lines on the skin of your palm and fingers. No matter the age of the specimen, the cap is most commonly bright yellow, sticky to the touch, and has a mildly fruity smell that can be compared to apricots. Occasionally, species with peach or coral-colored caps may be found, but these are less distinctive and trickier to identify.

The stem of the yellow-gilled russula is white, thick, and non-tapering—in other words, it does not get significantly narrower toward the top. The outer flesh of the stem, and the inner flesh of the entire mushroom, will not bruise gray when damaged. If a spore print is present, it should be a reddish ochre color.

The gills of the mushroom are yellow and attached to the stem at the base of the cap. Both the gills and the flesh of the entire mushroom are very fragile and delicate.

Where and When to Harvest

Yellow-gilled russulas are in season in summer and early fall—look for them after periods of warm weather. They may be growing in clusters, or scattered over a patch of ground, but are seldom found growing alone. The yellow-gilled russula almost entirely grows in the shade of hardwood trees, particularly the paper birch.

Uses

Like other russulas, the yellow-gilled russula has a mild, pleasant flavor, and is best sauteed in butter, broiled, or roasted. Adding salt—or even boiling in salted water before adding to a dish—is one way to enhance the mushroom's flavor.

Warnings and Lookalikes

While there are a number of other russula species in the PNW, there are no poisonous look-alikes for this specific mushroom that are difficult to distinguish. Just ensure that the specimen you're looking at has *all* of the traits described above, and if you're not sure, leave it alone.

Glistening Ink Cap (*Coprinellus micaceus*)

The glistening ink cap, also known as the mica cap, is a close relative and lookalike of the shaggy mane mushroom.

Physical Description

The cap of the glistening ink cap varies in size, but is always relatively small. Some sources give a size of around 2 inches (5 cm) in diameter (Kuo, 2008), but the size is missing from many other sources. The caps are ochre, yellow-brown, or beige, with a distinct extremely convex dome/umbrella shape that appears bulbous in younger specimens.

The caps of older specimens have black stains that resemble ink stains. By contrast, younger specimens are covered in small, bumpy granules. Another distinctive feature of the caps is their "radial groves" which extend from the centers to the rims. Caps may be covered with glistening particles that wash off easily.

The spore deposit, where present, is sooty black or gray-black. The stems are off-white or light beige, and are relatively long and skinny compared to the size and shape of the caps.

Where and When to Harvest

The glistening ink cap is most commonly found in Washington and British Columbia out of the regions in the PNW. It needs mild, rainy weather to grow best, so look for it especially in spring and fall.

Look for this mushroom at the base of trees—anywhere close to roots in the ground, whether they're living or dead. It may also grow on or near stumps of hardwood trees and other masses of decaying organic matter like dead leaves or animal dung.

Uses

The glistening ink cap needs to be cooked as soon as possible after harvesting—preferably within a few hours, or it *will* liquify. It has a very mild but pleasant flavor, and is commonly sauteed or stewed.

Warnings and Lookalikes

The glistening ink cap is a very short-lived mushroom, so if you spot a patch, don't assume you have time to come back and collect them another day! Furthermore, they *need* to be cooked within hours of harvesting, or will quickly liquify.

There are also several inedible lookalikes to this mushroom throughout the PNW.

- Two lookalike species, *Coprinopsis romagnesiana* and *Coprinopsis atramentaria,* can cause a negative reaction when combined with alcohol and are thought to be inedible regardless. The main way to distinguish them is that both species have dark brown or gray "scales" either in the center, or all over, their caps.

- *Coprinellus domesticus* has white scales on the caps and grows primarily on logs. Around the bases of the mushroom, orange hair-like fibers start to grow on the bark of the log.

- *Coprinellus floculocus* can be distinguished by the fuzzy white protrusions or "warts" that grow on its caps.

Horse Mushroom *(Agaricus arvensis)*

The horse mushroom got its name because it usually grows in fields, meadows, and pastures: Wide open spaces with plenty of grass where it makes sense for horses to graze! It may also be fertilized with horse dung and other animal dung.

Physical Description

The horse mushroom is a large mushroom with a classic cap-and-stem umbrella shape reminiscent of the king bolete. However, the cap only grows to around 7-8 inches in diameter max—still large compared to most mushrooms. The cap and stem are both white, yellow-white, or off-white, and should be smooth and dry to the touch. Older specimens have more and more of a yellow tinge as they age, and occasionally small brown scales appear in the center of the cap. The flesh is firm in texture, white, and does not immediately bruise when cut or damaged.

On the underside of the cap, you'll find thin, crowded gills that are pink in younger specimens and become dark brown or grayish-brown over time.

The stem is bulbous at the base, and decorated with a ring or skirt that is strong, not fluttery, and has a cogwheel-like pattern of notches around the outside. The stem is always smooth to the touch above the ring, but may be either smooth or scaly on the section below. On younger species, the skirt may still be attached as a partial veil, but it will still have that cogwheel pattern underneath.

Where present, the spore print will be a deep purple-brown, or brown with a purplish tint. It has a distinct smell similar to star anise.

Where and When to Harvest

The horse mushroom is in season June-December, though it can be found earlier in some warmer regions of the PNW.

As we mentioned above, the horse mushroom grows primarily in open, grassy spaces like pastures, meadows, and fields. But don't head out to a nearby patch of scraggly dry grass to look for horse mushrooms—they need a *fertile* field to grow properly, with plenty of nutrients in the soil!

You may also find horse mushrooms at the edges of woods, near hedgerows, and verges.

Uses

Horse mushrooms are the right size and texture to serve as a stand-in for portobello mushrooms. Thanks to their characteristic toughness, they can be sauteed, grilled, roasted, braised, and even broiled. They pair well with meat dishes and savory herbs, as well as olives, garlic, and strong cheeses. A spritz of lemon juice can help enhance their flavor.

Warnings and Lookalikes

Large, white mushrooms are fairly common, and so the horse mushroom has several lookalikes which are mostly inedible. Luckily, there are some simple ways to tell them apart:

- The lethally poisonous death cap (*Amanita phalloides*) has a narrower, more convex cap and lacks the characteristic cogwheel pattern on the skirt. The gills are white for the entire life cycle.
- The stem of the poisonous yellow stainer (*Agaricus xanthodermus*) stains bright yellow when cut, and may even leak yellow fluids.
- Other inedible lookalikes are found in the forest, while horse mushrooms are found in grassy fields. If there is no grass on the ground, or if you're surrounded by trees, assume what you're looking at is not a horse mushroom.
- Choosing larger specimens (over six inches in diameter across the cap) allows you to eliminate

some inedible species which are always smaller than that.

- All inedible lookalikes to the horse mushroom lack the characteristic cogwheel pattern, and many will quickly bruise when cut.

Never select horse mushrooms from fields where artificial fertilizer is used, as it can be present in the mushroom at levels unsafe for human consumption. If you're not *100%* sure, leave it alone.

If you look for horse mushrooms in places where livestock actually grazes, remember to respect private property and your local laws, as well as the personal space of any animals you encounter.

Western Giant Puffball (Calvatia gigantea)

The "giant" part of this fungus' name is no misnomer! Some of them can be larger than two feet across, if given enough time to grow in the right conditions.

Physical Description

As we stated above, the western giant puffball is a huge, round, white mushroom, up to 48 inches in diameter and sometimes even more in exceptional cases. The mushroom can be mistaken for a white ball at a distance, so if you see something that looks like a discarded volleyball in the woods, have a closer look!

There is no visible stalk or stem, and the outside of the mushroom is always white and fleshy when it's in the stage of the life cycle where it's edible, and the flesh inside should be white. Older specimens, which are not edible, have yellow, brown, or yellowish-brown flesh on the inside.

The western giant puffball has no external pores or gills, and instead produces its spores on the inside during the inedible mature stage. At the end of its life cycle it cracks to release spores.

Where and When to Harvest

Western giant puffballs are only edible during the juvenile stage. Depending on the location, the western giant puffball comes into season late in summer, and stays in season until the middle or end of autumn.

Look for these fungi at the borders between forests and meadows or fields, as well as at the edges of pastures and other open areas with rich, fertile soil. In rare cases, if the spot is open to the sky, they can grow inside forests.

The western giant puffball may grow alone or in patches. Sometimes, a group of specimens will form an eerie-looking circle!

Uses

There are historically-recorded medicinal uses for the western giant puffball. The Iroquois and Meskwaki peoples used it both for food and as a dressing for wounds, thanks to its styptic properties.

In terms of culinary uses, the mild flavor and absorbency of the western giant puffball makes it ideal for use in dishes with sauce or other flavorings, like pasta dishes, stir fries, and risottos. They can also be used as a substitute for chicken or tofu because of their firm texture and high protein content. They can also be breaded, deep fried, and served with dipping sauce.

While you *can* dry western giant puffballs to preserve them, just like other mushrooms, they don't respond as well to being dried and reconstituted in comparison to other species.

Warnings and Lookalikes

The western giant puffball is only edible when young. Older specimens are toxic, and taste horrible to boot! The flesh on the inside of the fungus should be pure white. If you see yellow or brown, assume it's too old. The outer skin of the mushroom should be removed before cooking.

You may occasionally find worms or larva when cutting open a puffball. If the infestation is located on a small portion of the fruiting body, you're fine to just cut that part out. But if you see discoloration throughout the body, or if the worms or larva are spread throughout, discard the specimen.

Because of the size and distinctive appearance of the western giant puffball, it's easy to distinguish from other white mushrooms. As it sometimes shares a habitat with the dreaded death caps, remember it does not have gills (especially not white gills) and is not raised off the ground by a stalk. Its round shape is the actual shape of the fruiting body and not the result of a universal or partial veil.

Common Puffball (Lycoperdon perlatum)

Don't let the unattractive spiky appearance of this savory treat turn you off! The common puffball has plenty of delicious uses. Fun fact: Another common name for the common puffball is "wolf fart"!

Physical Description

The common puffball is shaped like an upside-down pear, with a cap diameter between 1-3 inches. The top portion is rounded and bulbous, almost like a partially-veiled cap, while the stalk is seamlessly attached, thick, and sometimes short enough to be hard to notice. In the largest, tallest common puffballs, the fungi can reach a high of 3.5 inches or more.

Younger, smaller common puffballs are dry, soft, and white all over, while older and inedible specimens are tan, brown, or olive. Younger specimens are also covered in white or off-white spines that fall off as the specimen matures. Older puffballs lose their spines and develop a tougher outer skin as they mature, but on close examination have dimples or "scars" where the spines used to be. Where present, the spines are soft and pliable to the touch.

The inner flesh of a young puffball should be dry, soft, and pure white—one source compares it to the appearance and texture of marshmallows (Kitsap Peninsula Mycological Society, 2022). The flesh of older specimens darkens along with the rest of the body.

If present, the spore print is olive-brown.

Where and When to Harvest

Look for these fungi in the fall and winter—cool, wet weather is best for their life cycle! In cooler regions they can sometimes start to appear in late summer. The common puffball can be found growing alone, scattered over a patch, or even in tight clusters—without knowing the conditions in your area, it's hard to predict!

Common puffballs are very widespread, and can be found in open meadows, small groups of trees, and around the borders between forests and fields.

Uses

The taste of the common puffball is described with adjectives such as "earthy" and even "mushroom-y." The flavor is mild but distinct.

One interesting use of the common puffball is drying the fruiting body and then creating a powder, which is then used as a flavoring or seasoning for blander dishes. This powder can also be treated like bouillon and added to soup broths for an extra *oomph* of flavor and nutrition!

Otherwise, the absorbency of the common puffball's flesh makes it a great substitute for tofu, as it will quickly soak up sauces and oils during cooking. Common puffballs can also be added to pasta sauces, deep fried and served with dip, or sliced and added to pizzas—basically anywhere you'd put a store-bought cremini mushroom!

Extracts of the common puffball have been tested for a range of medical uses, and confirmed to help kill fungus and bacteria.

Warnings and Lookalikes

Like the western giant puffball, the common puffball is only edible when young, and when the inner flesh is still all-white.

The other issue is that since some poisonous *Aminata* species like destroying angels and death caps are both white and partially veiled when immature, they can take on a bulbous appearance that resembles a common puffball.

There is one surefire way to distinguish puffballs from poisonous look-alikes. The inside should be uniformly pure white and soft. Specifically, older puffball mushrooms or some similar-looking inedible species do not have pure white insides, while deadly *Amanita* species have the imprint of immature white gills and stems on the inside. If there's *any* kind of variation in texture, color, or pattern, discard the mushroom!

Note—make sure you individually check every single one of your puffballs in this way before cooking or eating them!

Slimy Spike Cap (Gomphidius glutinosus)

The "slime" that gives the slimy spike cap mushroom its name also gives it a distinctive glossy or glistening appearance. Combined with the shape of the mushroom, the slimy spike cap can be said to look like an old-fashioned spinning top toy!

Physical Description

The cap is about 5 inches in diameter in larger specimens, and fawn, dull purple, purple-brown, dull brown, brown-gray, or dark brown in color. In older specimens, the cap may have black splotches or marks. The cap is convex in shape with a raised center and "in-rolled" rims. The shape of the cap becomes flatter/less convex and more and more irregular as the mushroom matures.

Younger slimy spike caps are completely veiled with sticky, slimy membrane that gives them their distinct shiny appearance, while older specimens have only a skirt left in the middle of the stem. Remnants of the veil may be left on the rest of the mushroom even after this stage of the life cycle. Caps remain shiny and slimy to the touch after the veil breaks. The raised center of the cap may feel spiky to the touch.

Underneath the cap you'll find wide-spaced gills that range in color from off-white to gray or (in older specimens) purple-gray.

The stem is up to four inches tall, and relatively skinny compared to the cap (under an inch in diameter). The color of the stem is white or off-white, darkening to gray-brown toward the bottom, and sometimes tinged or stained bright yellow around the base. The stem should also be covered in slime.

The inner flesh of the mushroom is white or off-white and may take a plum or wine-colored tinge. Where present, the spore print is dark brown-black. You may also find brown-black or black staining on the gills of older specimens from the spores.

Where and When to Harvest

The slimy spike cap is in season in fall and winter. In unusual regions, fruiting bodies start to sprout as early as June. The slimy spike cap thrives at both high and low elevations, and so can be found on the slopes of hills or mountains so long as the right trees are present.

Look for these unusual mushrooms in the PNW's conifer forests. Slimy spike caps are *always* found around the roots of conifers, especially spruce. They may be growing alone, in small clusters, or scattered over a patch.

Uses

The slimy spike cap is safe to eat, but one problem is that it has little flavor. It is also not suitable for drying unlike most other mushrooms, and can't be cooked whole as the outer layer of slime is not considered edible.

However, that doesn't mean this unusual fungus is useless! The slimy spike cap is best skinned, cut up and used in dishes where it is not intended to be the star of the show, but where there's a place for a subtle mushroom-y taste and texture. It may also be added to dishes where a mix of different mushroom species are used, like mushroom ravioli or mushroom-stuffed peppers.

One plus side to the slimy spike cap that makes it a little more appetizing is that this mushroom is very unlikely to be infested with maggots or worms when you find it in the wild—the characteristic slime serves to protect the mushroom from parasites!

Warnings and Lookalikes

The slime that makes these mushrooms so distinctive is primarily composed of gluten, which many people are allergic to or unable to properly digest. Whether or not you can tolerate gluten, you should remove the outer layer of the mushroom, including the slime as it can cause indigestion and gas.

The slimy spike cap does have lookalikes, but these can be easily distinguished. Most are edible but are unpleasant-tasting.

- The bitter sticky bun mushroom (*Sullius luteus*) looks extremely similar, but has pores under the cap instead of gills.
- The herald of winter (*Hygrophorus hypothejus*) looks similar and shares a similar season, but has distinctly yellow gills.
- The insidious gomphidius (*Gomphidius oregonensis*) is similar in season, locale, and appearance. It can be distinguished by the close-spacing of the gills, and the shape and color of the cap (pink, salmon, or fawn in younger specimens and purple- or red-brown in mature specimens, with the cap getting increasingly concave and depressed at the center as the specimen ages).

Western Saffron Milk Cap (*Lactarius deliciosus*)

Also known as the "delicious milk cap," this is one of the tastiest mushrooms in the entire PNW! The mushroom produces milky latex fluid when squeezed or broken, hence the "milk" part of the name.

Physical Description

The classically convex-shaped cap has a diameter of 2 to 6 inches in most specimens, and is either pink-orange or a warm orange-yellow color reminiscent of saffron. The shape of the cap becomes more irregular and wavier as the mushroom matures, and eventually develops a depression in the middle, creating a donut-like shape. On close examination, the color of the cap is not uniform but covered in concentric rings of various orange-yellow shades.

Turning over the cap you'll find crowded gills that are pinkish-tan, tan, or orange and that break apart easily when manipulated. They may be stained green from latex in older specimens.

The stem and the inner flesh of the mushroom are both pale off-white mottled with pale pink in younger specimens, and gradually take on more of an orange hue as the mushroom matures. The stem may be entirely cylindrical, or may get narrower toward the base, and is always hollow inside when cut open.

The latex secreted by the mushroom is orange in younger specimens and greenish in older specimens. All parts of the mushroom bruise green when damaged. There is no visible ring or veil.

The outer texture of the mushroom is "crunchy" and breaks with an audible *snap*, especially in older specimens.

Where and When to Harvest

The western saffron milk cap is in season from early spring through late fall, and found in the coniferous forests of the PNW, where it forms symbiotic relationships with the roots of coniferous trees.

Since the season is so broad, it can be hard to figure out exactly when to look for these delicious mushrooms. The best rule of thumb is to go out just a couple days after a heavy rain while the mushroom is in season, and poke around the bases of evergreen trees, particularly pines.

Hint—since these mushrooms aren't very tall, they may be buried under twigs, needles, and other debris around the base of conifers! They may also blend in with fallen autumn leaves because of their own orange color.

Uses

The color of the western saffron milk cap is very aesthetically pleasing, which makes it very appetizing! It's also described as being extremely tasty when cooked. You can use the western saffron milk cap for basically anything where you'd use another flavorful mushroom. They have a meaty, chewy texture when cooked, and a savory flavor that pairs well with grilled meats, onions, herbs, garlic, olives, and seafood.

Be aware that if you're adding the western saffron milk cap to a liquid-based dish, like a stew, soup, pasta sauce, or curry, the "milk" produced by the mushroom will color the liquid orange. Sometimes the saffron milk cap is *deliberately* chosen as an ingredient for this reason!

Thanks to their striking color, these mushrooms make great additions to open-faced sandwiches, pizzas, and flatbreads.

Warnings and Lookalikes

The easiest way to distinguish this species from lookalikes is the latex, or fluid, it secretes when cut or squeezed. As we mentioned above, the latex should be orange in younger specimens and take on a greenish color as the mushroom matures.

Lactarius deterrimus, or the false saffron milk cap, is edible but bitter tasting. It can be distinguished by its less vibrant coloring, which takes on a grayish tinge over the orange.

Meadow Mushroom (Agaricus campestris)

This gorgeous mushroom is very similar to the horse mushroom profiled above, and even occupies the same *Agaricus* genus! Another close relative is the "button" mushroom you can find at the grocery store.

Physical Description

The fruiting body of the meadow mushroom takes a classic umbrella shape with a distinct cap and stem. With the exception of the gills, the entire outside of most meadow mushrooms is white, off-white, or cream, possibly tinged with brown. Some older specimens turn brown all over, but this doesn't always happen. The flesh should have a smooth, dry texture on the outside in all specimens, and a firm texture on the inside. The color of the inner flesh is also white, sometimes tinged with brown, and is known to have a pleasant odor.

The cap is smaller than in other *Agaricus* mushrooms, with a maximum diameter of four inches in most cases. It has a convex shape which grows steadily flatter as the mushroom matures.

Immature fruiting bodies have a spherical appearance due to their partial veil, which is white and smooth. When the mushroom outgrows and breaks through the veil, it forms a ring in the middle of the stem, which remains white at first and then turns brown with age.

The most distinctive aspect of the meadow mushroom's appearance is the pink gills—these are usually around the color of raw salmon in younger specimens. As the mushroom matures, the gills fade to grayish brown, brown, or black. In all specimens the gills are crowded and not attached to the stem.

The stem of the mushroom is white, cylindrical, and decorated with a ring. It is smooth above the ring and covered in loose hairs or "fibrils" below. When damaged, the stem will bruise off-white or eventually dull brown, but should *never* bruise or stain another color.

Where and When to Harvest

Meadow mushrooms are in season in spring, summer, and fall. Look for them the same places you would look for horse mushrooms—fields, pastures, meadows, lawns, and other fertile wide open spaces!

Tip: Meadow mushrooms commonly (but not always) grow in rings! This can help you spot them at a distance.

Uses

Meadow mushrooms have a mild, pleasant, savory taste that is similar to store-bought button mushrooms—but better! Therefore, they can be used virtually anywhere you would use a button mushroom—soups, stews, pasta sauces, sandwiches, and so on.

In Italian cuisine, button mushrooms, meadow mushrooms, and similar species are used in sauteed dishes with olive oil, herbs, garlic, onions, and tomatoes. There is also an Italian practice of marinating mushrooms, where mushrooms are simmered in a mix of olive oil, lemon juice, bay leaves, salt, and the mushroom's own juices before being placed in a jar with the mixture to marinate. Marinated mushrooms are served as a side to meat dishes or as part of an *antipasto* tray.

Meadow mushrooms pair well with acidic flavors like lemon and vinegar as well as savory herbs, beef, venison, poultry, and full-bodied red wines.

Warnings and Lookalikes

Agaricus genus mushrooms are a little trickier than the others on this list to identify in the PNW—reason being they have numerous lookalikes, some of which are poisonous. It's important to remember that different types of mushroom can also be mixed together in a field, so if you find one that looks good, don't assume all the mushrooms around it are also safe! Here's how to distinguish meadow mushrooms from inedible lookalikes:

- Ensure that the mushroom does not stain or bruise any bright color as soon as it is cut. As we said above, these mushrooms may stain off-white when damaged (fading to brownish over time), but if you see red, blue, orange, or yellow, it's not a meadow mushroom.

- Ensure the gills are pink—while they do turn brown with age, it's easiest to identify younger specimens whose gills are still pink.
  - If the mushroom is still veiled, you should be able to see pink when you slice it open.
  - The gills should be a clear salmon pink. Pinkish-brown doesn't cut it!
  - *Especially* beware of lookalikes with white gills—these are either the death cap or destroying angel, both of them lethally poisonous.
- Put a size cap on the mushrooms you pick. Meadow mushrooms are almost always under four inches in diameter, while some other species look similar but grow larger.

Red Cracked Bolete (Boletus chrysenteron)

The red cracked bolete isn't famous for its underwhelming taste and texture, but for being an incredibly widespread species throughout the PNW!

Physical Description

The cap of the red cracked bolete reaches a diameter of up to four and a half inches and as in other kinds of boletes takes a convex shape. The cap gets gradually flatter as the mushroom ages, becoming as flat as a plate in the oldest specimens. The color of the cap is mostly gray-brown or dark brown, decorated with paler cracks in the outer skin that give this mushroom the "cracked" part of its name. The "red" part comes from the bright pink coloring of damaged parts of the cap, which take on a red tinge.

The red cracked bolete does not have gills, and instead spreads its spores via large yellowish pores found under the cap.

The stem of the red cracked bolete is beige, dingy yellow, or dull yellow, and takes on an S-shaped curved appearance. The outside of the stem is usually streaked or tinged with red, sometimes intensely enough to conceal most of the yellow underneath.

The flesh is usually white, but gradually becomes more reddish closer to the skin. The flesh bruises blue or blue-green slowly when cut or damaged. If you see bruising on the flesh immediately, this is a sign it isn't a red-cracked bolete. The gills bruise more easily than the flesh, and in the same colors.

Where and When to Harvest

The red cracked bolete is in season throughout the year with the exception of winter, and is easiest to find when you know where to look. This mushroom primarily grows close to the roots of conifer or hardwood trees, with which it forms a symbiotic relationship. It appears to prefer conifers overall, but will also thrive on the roots of beeches, a common hardwood in the PNW. Therefore, look for the red cracked bolete in areas with plenty of tree coverage from these species!

Another way to spot this mushroom is the way it grows. Red cracked boletes are perfectly happy to grow alone, but you will more likely find many scattered around the roots of the same stand. Red cracked boletes are widespread and common throughout the PNW, so you may not have to look far before you find these!

Uses

The red cracked bolete is edible, and there are plenty of them….but the taste is mild, and described by some as "not distinctive" (O'Reilly, 2016). There's also the issue of the texture, which is reportedly soggy and unpleasant.

Try cooking the red cracked bolete with whichever methods you'd use for any other soft vegetable like an eggplant—not everyone dislikes it! Other ideas include mixing the red cracked bolete with other mushrooms and vegetables to stretch the size of a soup or stir fry, or cutting it up into small pieces and using it in a strongly flavored soup or curry.

Warnings and Lookalikes

There are many edible lookalikes to the red cracked bolete in the PNW, but there are also many *inedible* lookalikes. The key to telling the difference is to remember three simple rules:

- There are pores, not gills, under the cap, and the pores are always yellow in color, *never* red or orange.
- The flesh should bruise blue or blue-green when cut or damaged, *never* any other color. Also, the bruising process should be slow. If a vibrant blue color appears immediately, you have the wrong fungus!
- The mushroom should not have a foul smell or taste—if so, it's not a red cracked bolete.

There are also two more safety notes to consider with this mushroom:

- The red cracked bolete is particularly susceptible to mold. If you find one infected with fluffy white mold, don't just cut the mold off—assume the entire thing is now inedible.
- The red cracked bolete's pores are close to the ground, and very absorbent. Be aware of any risk of contamination, and never assume something is okay if you have doubts.

Jelly Ear Mushroom (Auricularia auricula)

This odd-looking but perfectly edible mushroom is also known as the wood ear, because it appears to be an ear growing out of the side of a tree!

Physical Description

The jelly ear mushroom grows on the side of a tree, and so does not take the characteristic umbrella shape of most mushrooms. Instead, it can most-simply be described as ear-shaped! The fruiting body is a convex semi-circle that gets wavier with age. The rims turn in toward the center of the body, just like the cartilage in our ears, and are as thin as paper.

Older specimens that have an increasingly wavy, crinkly appearance can look more like brains, especially since a distinctive characteristic of the jelly ear is that fruiting bodies grow in tangled, overlapping clusters.

The color of the fruiting body is brown and may get darker with age. The appearance is translucent—the sun will shine through it at the right angle—with a visual effect similar to, you guessed it, light shining through the thin skin of someone's ear.

You may find a jelly ear looking completely black and dried out. This doesn't alter the edibility—you can just reconstitute it like you would if you'd dried the mushroom yourself!

The texture of the jelly ear is, as the name suggests, jelly-like, but you should not be able to squash it effortlessly. The fruiting body of a true jelly ear will hold its shape and return to it when you try to flatten it out. However, you should be able to *fold* the mushroom as easily as you would a blanket or towel, and should not crack or break when folded.

The jelly ear mushroom can be found in either temperate rainforests or conifer forests, and is in season in fall and winter. Look for this mushroom especially after cold, wet weather.

As we stated above, look for jelly ear mushrooms on the sides of trees. While they can grow perfectly well on living or dead wood, one way to spot trees bearing these savory treats is to look for trees that appear to be sick, dying, or damaged. The jelly ear mushroom is a parasite, and weaker trees are especially susceptible.

Keep an eye out for the many variations jelly ear mushrooms display in their appearances! Older specimens may not have the distinct half-cup shape anymore, if they've gotten too crinkly. Also, since jelly ears grow mixed-up together in a tight colony with individual fruiting bodies passing through or under their neighbors, it's easy to pass over an absolute treasure trove if you don't look closer! Check out any mass of brown or black fungi stuck to the side of a tree, and use an up-close view of the shape, color, *and* texture to determine if it's what you're looking for.

Uses

The jelly ear mushroom is also widespread in Asia, and is a common part of many Asian cuisines! In China, jelly ears are called "black fungus." Jelly ears are perfectly suited for the flavors that come with Chinese-inspired dishes, especially the tangy mix of sweet, spicy, and sour found in hot and sour soup—a Chinese dish that traditionally uses dried jelly ears as a star ingredient.

These fungi pair well with a range of flavors, including pork, chicken, fermented black beans, soy sauce, red wine vinegar and rice wine vinegar, sesame oil, various savory herbs including parsley and cilantro, onions, potatoes, shallots, ginger, and garlic. Choose savory, salty ingredients to accompany the mushrooms and help them shine.

The field of Traditional Chinese Medicine uses jelly ear mushrooms to lower blood pressure, manage high blood sugar, and fight blood clots.

Warnings and Lookalikes

The great thing about the jelly ear mushroom is that you are unlikely to mistake anything else for this *extremely* unique-looking fungus!

Hedgehog Mushroom (Hydnum sp.)

This group of silly-looking fungi is actually closely related to the Pacific golden chanterelle!

Physical Description

The hedgehog mushroom is actually a group of closely related species, all of them perfectly edible and tasty—we'll address how you can distinguish any mushrooms that aren't part of this group in the last section of this entry!

The biggest variation between the mushrooms that fall under this umbrella is the cap color. Depending on your region and the species, you can find hedgehog mushrooms with caps that are yellow-orange, orange, dull yellow, beige, tan, fawn, salmon pink, brown, and off-white or sometimes even pure white. In all species the cap is smooth and dry in texture, but may start cracking and becoming more and more irregular as the mushrooms grow and push against the other mushrooms in the cluster. Overall, the shape of the cap is irregularly planar. Some species have a depression in the middle of the cap.

The most distinctive unifying feature of hedgehog mushrooms is the "teeth" or spines under the caps, which are crowded close together. Hedgehog mushrooms *always* have these instead of pores or gills. The teeth are off-white or cream in color.

The stem of the mushroom can be solid *or* hollow depending on the subspecies, but is always irregular and curved. The flesh is white and has a pleasant odor. Where present, the spore print is always pale cream or white.

Here are two species of hedgehog mushroom in the Pacific Northwest:

Hydnum umbilicatum

- warm orange, tan-orange or tan in color over the entire fruiting body
- small cap, usually under 2 inches in diameter
- short, hollow stem
- key feature: small depression in the middle of the cap that looks like a belly-button

Hydnum albomagnum

- similar in color to the previous two species but paler, usually looking light yellow or yellow-orange, beige, or cream
- stem is also pale beige, cream, or off-white

- larger cap, sometimes up to the size of a full dinner plate
- no depression in the cap

Where and When to Harvest

Hedgehog mushrooms are in season from summer through to fall, though the exact dates depend on your local climate. Where to look for hedgehog mushrooms depends on the species. All of these mushrooms form symbiotic relationships with trees, and are found in the forest around tree roots.

H. umbilicatum is always found around conifers in coniferous forests, primarily pines. Less information about which kinds of trees *H. albomagnum* grows beside is available, but overall, members of the *Hydnum* group of species can grow in either temperate rainforests or conifer forests, and oak trees appear to be the preferred symbiote.

Hedgehog mushrooms of any species or subspecies can be singular, scattered, or grow in a ring, but oftentimes grow in *very* dense clusters that are noticeable from a distance. These clusters are so close together sometimes that the caps of the individual fruiting bodies become cracked and damaged from crowding!

Uses

Hedgehog mushrooms can be described as sweet, slightly bitter, or peppery. They are well-suited to being dried and reconstituted, which makes them a welcome addition to soups, stews, sauces, and other liquid-based dishes.

Hedgehog mushrooms pair well with meat dishes like steak, as they have a distinct flavor that can stand up on its own. A few cracks of black pepper can also make the peppery flavor of the mushrooms stand out even more.

H. albomagnum and some other larger species are big and solid enough to brush with olive oil and throw on a grill or barbecue! These can be served as a meat substitute or side, with whatever condiments or seasonings you like on your barbecue fare.

The *H. umbilicatum* has a distinctly sweet taste and fruity odor reminiscent of the Pacific golden chanterelle, so refer to the "uses" guide for that species for even more tips on how to prepare these!

One last note? While you should always check and make sure to clean your mushrooms, hedgehog mushrooms are highly unlikely to be infested with bugs, worms, or maggots!

Warnings and Lookalikes

We chose the *H. umbilicatum* and the *H. albomagnum* to highlight because of their distinctive features—the "belly button" and their very large size, respectively. However, there are no inedible hedgehog mushrooms.

Apricot Jelly Mushroom (Guepinia helvelloides)

The apricot jelly mushroom is one of the most beautiful mushrooms in the Pacific Northwest!

Physical Description

The shape of the jelly is elongated, usually irregular, and can be likened to a tongue, flower, or leaf. It curves to form a hollow funnel that can even resemble a golden chanterelle at a distance. The edges curve away from the hollow inside of the fruiting body, and can be wavy at the edges, especially in older specimens. The outside of the mushroom may be decorated with noticeable wrinkles— think of the surface of a brain or the criss-crossing veins under a person's tongue.

The color of the fruiting body is pinkish orange, salmon pink, or apricot. The texture is jelly-like but distinctly dry and rubbery. If you hold a specimen up to the sun (or just shine your phone flashlight through it), you should be able to see light shining through.

The stem of the apricot jelly is streamlined with the rest of the mushroom and the same color, but the fruiting body narrows and becomes paler (even yellow-white or off-white) toward the base. If present, spore prints are white.

Where and When to Harvest

Apricot jelly mushrooms are in season in summer and fall. They are found growing in very specific conditions—on rotting wood (or more rarely on soil full of fertile rotting wood debris), in conifer forests. Apricot jellies grow singularly, in small groups, or in beautiful, crowded clusters that resemble bouquets.

Tip: Remember these fungi-like wood that is in an advanced stage of decay and thus partially buried and disintegrated. You might not notice the log itself, so look out for that telltale lively orange color!

Uses

The taste of the apricot jelly fungus is mildly sweet to indistinct. Add this to too strongly flavored of a dish, and it will disappear into the background! However, the lack of a strong flavor doesn't mean this fungus is useless!

Because of the lack of a distinct flavor combined with the bright colors and pleasant appearance of the mushroom, it can be pickled, marinated, fermented, or candied in order to imbue it with an acidic taste that will enhance the natural flavor of the mushroom. Pickled apricot jelly could be an interesting accompaniment to any sandwich, burger, salad, sushi, and so on where other pickled vegetables would be used! If you're not a fan of pickles, the beautiful color of the mushroom makes it a welcome addition to open-faced sandwiches, pizzas, and flatbreads.

Warnings and Lookalikes

There are absolutely no lookalikes to this mushroom in the Pacific Northwest, making it one of the safest mushrooms for beginner foragers to confidently identify! However, make sure to practice rattlesnake safety when exploring around logs.

Lion's Mane Mushroom (Hericium erinaceus)

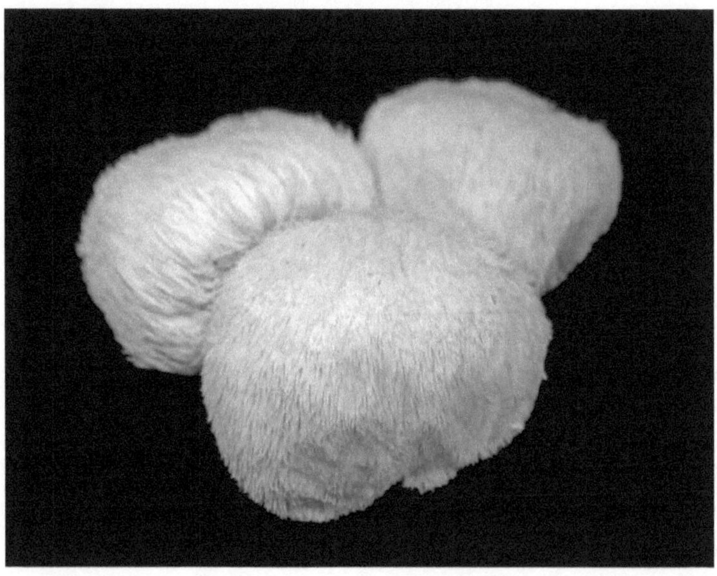

Fun fact—the *Hericium* in the scientific name of this striking mushroom is actually a reference to hedgehogs, as their spines remind some naturalists of porcupine quills!

Physical Description

The lion's mane mushroom grows on damaged, exposed wood. It takes the appearance of a large puff or tuft of white tendrils, which hang downwards toward the ground like a beard. The entire fruiting body of the fungus is white, with each individual spine being up to 2 inches long and the diameter of the fruiting body being up to 15 inches across, larger than a dinner plate! The shape of the body is a squashed circular or ovular blob, and the appearance of the mushroom can be said to resemble a cheerleader's pom-pom.

If you were to remove a lion's mane from a tree, you'd find a firm, white body anchoring it to the bark—but this should not be visible in general. The inner flesh of the mushroom is white and solid.

As the mushroom ages, the tendrils start to show signs of wear, damage, and yellowing. They are also "droopier" in older specimens.

Where and When to Harvest

Lion's mane mushrooms are in season from late summer into fall, but specifically you want to keep an eye out for them growing on damaged, felled, or split hardwood trees where the inner wood is exposed—this is where the lion's mane likes to grow.

If you want a tip for finding these gigantic vegetables when you're searching the PNW's rainforests for mushrooms? A few days after a major rainstorm with wind, thunder, and lightning, take a walk and look for trees that were knocked down by the wind or split open from lightning! Come back to these periodically to see if you get lucky—if one of the damaged trees you found sprouts a lion's mane, you don't want to miss out on that treat!

Uses

There is data to suggest the lion's mane mushroom has some brain-boosting properties: It has a mild effect in countering anxiety and depression, as well as a potential protective effect against dementia and may even slow the progress of neurological disorders, and boost recovery from neurological injuries (Julson, 2018).

The flavor of the lion's mane mushroom is described as mild, light, and pleasant. Sometimes, it has been compared to crab, lobster, or other seafood for its mild, slightly sweet taste and texture. It pairs with light white wines, fresh salads with sweet, citrusy dressings (the mushroom must be cooked to be edible) and other ingredients that go well with seafood. Based on the white color, mildly sweet taste, and long, "noodly" look, it's possible that lion's mane could serve as a stand-in for enoki mushrooms.

Warnings and Lookalikes

Like many of the mushrooms on this list, the great thing about the lion's mane is that it doesn't really have lookalikes in the entire Pacific Northwest—at least not any that could be mistaken for it! Here is a short list of things to double-check just to be sure:

- no foul smell
- growing on exposed, damaged wood
- no visible stem attaching it to the tree
- white all over

Fairy Ring Mushroom (Marasmius oreades)

There is a common historical superstition that fairies would hold dances at rings of mushrooms in the woods, and that a careless mortal who steps inside a fairy ring risks getting stolen away!

Physical Description

The cap has a diameter of 2 inches or less. It is "bell shaped" with a flared-out rim and a raised center, reminiscent of an old-fashioned church bell. In younger specimens, the cap is convex, but becomes gradually flatter as the mushroom grows. According to Alan Bergo, an expert on cooking with foraged plants, it's easier to describe the shape of the cap as resembling a human nipple—and he's right! Along with the shape, caps of fairy ring mushrooms become more irregular and wrinkled as they mature. The cap is delicate in texture and wrinkles with age, which just increases its nipple-esque appearance!

The cap and stem of the mushroom is a neutral medium-brown, tan, ochre, cream, buff, or orangish-brown color. The stem may be darker at the base.

Underneath the cap you'll find gills that are similar in color to the rest of the mushroom, relatively widely spaced, and usually forked around the rim of the cap. These are very pale, white, or off-white in young specimens, but which quickly darken to cream or buff as the mushroom matures. The color of the gills usually closely resembles the color of the rest of the mushroom.

The stems of fairy ring mushrooms are very strong, but pliable. You should be able to pick a specimen and then tug and bend the stem back and forth without breaking it—in fact, you're more likely to rip the more delicate cap by accident than you are to pull the stem clean off or break it.

While the cap's skin is delicate and the stem's is not, the entire fruiting body should be smooth and dry to the touch. Where present, the spore print is white.

Where and When to Harvest

The season for fairy ring mushrooms starts in spring, and extends into late fall or early winter. Seek out fairy ring mushrooms when the weather has been cool and damp, especially if it's rained.

The most distinctive thing about fairy mushrooms in the wild is that they usually grow in a congruent ring (though they may also be scattered across a patch—never solitary). Look for these mushrooms in places with plenty of sun, particularly meadows, fields, livestock pastures, and even yards and lawns! Fairy ring mushrooms are most likely to grow in a circle around a decaying tree stump, or if the stump was removed, the crater or hole where the stump used to be. They especially like to grow on top of a "brulee" or a dark-colored ring of grass surrounding decaying matter.

Note: Many, *many* species of mushroom can grow in rings, but fairy ring mushrooms are more often found in this arrangement than not. Some expert foragers report that fruiting bodies sprout from the same place, and presumably the same mycelium, every year (Bergo, 2015).

Uses

Fairy ring mushrooms' biggest culinary strength is how easy they are to dry! These mushrooms essentially dry and reconstitute themselves repeatedly throughout their life cycle.

Since they will re-absorb liquid with ease, fairy ring mushrooms are perfect for pasta sauces, soups, and stews. They also make a great addition to omelets, where they enhance the sweeter flavors of fried onions.

Fairy ring mushrooms are high in a sugar called trehalose. While their taste is described as earthy, nutty, and mushroom-y, they are also sweeter-tasting than other kinds of wild mushroom. We suggest avoiding strong-tasting ingredients that will overpower their unique flavor. For example, if you wanted to add them to a pasta sauce, consider trying a subtle cream sauce with some savory herbs in the mix to help their sweetness stand out!

Some suggested pairings include bright white wines, cognac, pork, seafood, fresh herbs, and butter.

Warnings and Lookalikes

A *lot* of inedible mushrooms are small, brown, and grow in rings—there are so many lookalikes it wouldn't be practical to go through them all here. However, you don't need a degree in mycology or a microscope to positively identify the delicious fungi you're chasing. Here's how to distinguish fairy ring mushrooms from inedible lookalikes:

- Always do a stem test—pick a specimen and try to wrap the stem around your finger like a ring. If the stem breaks, it is *not* a fairy ring mushroom.

- The stem is *always* solid on the inside—some inedible lookalikes have hollow stems.
- Remember that these mushrooms will not grow deep in the woods—they need sun to thrive!
- There should be a subtle "sawdust" smell detectable close-up, but the mushroom should not have a stinky or pungent order.

Two more quick warnings:

- These mushrooms are super absorbent. If you find them growing near roads or highways, or in a field where artificial pesticides or fertilizers have been used, assume they're contaminated and not fit for consumption.
- Worms *love* to attack fairy ring mushrooms. Before gathering mushrooms from a ring you've found, pick a specimen and cut the cap in half. If you see small holes in the flesh, it means worms have infested the fruiting body, and you should consider the whole ring or patch inedible.

Comb Toothed Fungus (Hericium coralloides)

This delicate branching fungus resembles snow covering tree branches—and tastes much better!

Physical Description

The comb toothed mushroom's fruiting body is entirely white, off-white, or cream, does not have a typical cap and stem shape, but is instead a collection of "branches" that form a blob-shaped or ovular mass that only grows on dead trees and logs. The flesh gets darker as the fungus ages. The branches are not attached to each other on the outside— you can put your hand in between the gaps. The fruiting body of one comb-toothed fungus reaches a rough diameter of around 4-16 inches.

The branches of the comb toothed fungus are covered in short spines that are around a third of an inch in length. While they won't cut you, they give the branches a coarse, rough texture. By contrast, the inner flesh of the mushroom is soft to the touch, but not pliable—it will break if bent. Like the outside, the inner flesh is white to cream in color.

While it's hard to see this fungus' stem, it does have one, which is short and stubby. If you reach in and touch the stem, you'll find it's covered in hair-like protrusions. Where present, the spore print is white.

Where and When to Harvest

The comb toothed fungus is in season from late summer until late fall. In warmer areas of the Pacific Northwest, they can also occur earlier in summer or spring, or persist later into winter.

Look out for these beautiful fungi in the PNW's temperate rainforests, as they primarily grow on the wood of dead or dying conifers, as well as on damaged living trees whose inner wood has been exposed (such as by animal scratches or a storm), rotting logs and even fallen sticks and branches. It's possible that the comb-toothed fungus can also grow on conifers, but the evidence for this is dubious.

Tip: When these gorgeous fungi grow side by side, they can create a huge mass! These are easy to spot at a distance.

Uses

The comb toothed fungus is known for having a nutty taste, which is delicate and not overpowering. Its easily breakable texture makes it a nice addition to soups and other soft dishes, though it can be cooked and added to virtually anything if you don't like a ton of bite in your mushroom.

This versatile fungus also has medicinal properties according to proponents of herbal medicine. It may be used to calm stomach pain and boost the immune system in order to fight colds, stomach bugs, and other minor illnesses.

Warnings and Lookalikes

The closest two lookalikes to this mushroom, the bear's tooth fungus and the lion's mane fungus, are both edible.

The comb toothed fungus is only edible when young. Choose a small specimen and be sure the flesh on both the inside and outside are still pure white. Not only can an older, cream-colored fungus give you stomach trouble, but they're also said to be very sour-tasting.

Furthermore, some species of small beetle like to live inside the comb toothed fungus. Give it a good hard shake when you harvest it to reduce how many you carry home, and cut open and closely examine each specimen before eating.

Yellow Swamp Russula (Russula claroflava)

Not to be confused with the yellow-gilled russula, this species is also known as the yellow swamp brittlegill.

Physical Description

The yellow swamp russula, as the name suggests, has a bright mustard yellow cap, which reaches diameters of up to 4 inches across. In younger specimens, the caps are round and convex, but start to get more and more flat as the mushroom ages until they turn inside out from their old position and get concave! Before this happens, a depression appears in the center of the cap. The caps are shiny and smooth most of the time, but take on a sticky texture when they've been rained on.

Underneath the cap, the gills are crowded, long, and off-white to pale ochre.

The stem and inner flesh of the mushroom are white, but bruise gray very slowly when damaged. The stem is completely smooth with no ring, and fades to grayish-white as the mushroom ages. The texture of the flesh is firm and solid.

The spore print of the yellow swamp russula is pale ochre.

Where and When to Harvest

Look for these mushrooms in summer to fall, though depending on the climate of the region they may be able to grow outside of that time. Despite the name "swamp" these mushrooms are not found in the middle of saturated bogs. Instead, look for them around aspens and birches, trees that grow near the edges of some of the PNW's essential wetlands. If you're in a damp, marshy area but the ground is still firm enough to walk over, *and* you see aspens or birches, start looking for this mushroom!

Uses

The yellow swamp russula's flavor has been described as mild but "hot" by some—making it an excellent addition to dishes like curries where a good deal of heat is expected! Alternatively, use this mushroom in dishes where you wouldn't necessarily expect to find heat, but where they would really shine—for example, sauteed mushrooms and onions are a common topping for steak in some parts of the world, and a mushroom that comes with some heat would be ideal for this! Due to their firm flesh, they can be tossed into soups and stews, and also make a great addition to omelets. Their flavor is also known to pair well with garlic.

Warnings and Lookalikes

The only mistakeable lookalike to the yellow swamp russula is the ochre brittlegill, which is also edible and looks extremely similar except that the color of the cap is more ochre than yellow!

Beware that if the nearby swamps or wetlands are polluted, the nearby yellow swamp russula probably are too.

Shaggy Mane Mushroom (Coprinus comatus)

In *Practical Self Reliance*, a blog about homesteading and foraging, expert forager Ashley Adamant describes these mushrooms as absolutely foolproof for beginners to identify! She also notes that they resemble the "old school wigs from historical courtrooms" (2018).

Physical Description

The cap of the shaggy mane mushroom is elongated, and sometimes conical. The caps are covered in scales that turn up at the edges, from which the shaggy hair-like protrusions that give these mushrooms their name grow. While the cap itself is white or grayish white, the scales (or the hairs at their edges) are sometimes grayish, reddish-brown, or tan/light reddish-brown.

The gills of the mushroom are white in very young specimens, but stain black as soon as the mushroom starts to age. The black gills should stain your hand when you touch them, and in older specimens the cap will stain your hands black as well. You will sometimes see this "ink" in a puddle under an older specimen!

The flesh is white, soft, and *extremely* delicate, getting more fragile with age. In fact, younger specimens are the only ones you can easily harvest because older specimens will just fall apart in your hands!

The stem, like the cap, is white or grayish white with hairs on the outside, and hollow on the inside. They are relatively thin and get narrower toward the cap. The inside of the stem resembles a straw or tube because it's so round and even.

Where and When to Harvest

Shaggy mane mushrooms are in season from late summer through the fall. They grow on soil that has been regularly disturbed, treated, compacted, or otherwise altered. You can find them in gardens, on lawns, wood mulch, or on the edges of well-trafficked hiking trails. They also appear in weedy patches of grass. These mushrooms are often found alone, but occasionally you'll see them scattered over a small patch.

Uses

These mushrooms are difficult to cook with because they *really* degrade quickly. They need to be used pretty much the same day you pick them, preferably within a couple of hours. However, the black ink of the mushroom—if you harvest a few and let them degrade a little—can be used as a natural food coloring! Otherwise, they can still be cooked and added to soups or any other dish where you don't need the mushroom to be firm or keep its shape.

Warnings and Lookalikes

Shaggy mane mushrooms are "foolproof" in that they are incredibly unique looking, and easily distinguished from their only two lookalikes, the common inky cap (*Coprinus atramentarius*) and the mica cap/glistening ink cap (*Coprinellus micaceus*). The shaggy scales are not present on either of these species. The common inky cap causes a negative reaction when mixed with alcohol, so some avoid drinking while consuming them. If you are sure what species you have—which you should be 100% of the time—this isn't a problem!

Section 3:

From Forest to Table:

Enjoying Your Harvest

In this section, we're going to go over the best ways to harvest mushrooms in the wild, and what equipment you need to do it right. We'll also give you some tips on cooking your mushrooms, preserving them by dehydration, and some basic recipes to get you started!

The Forager's Backpack: What You Need to Bring

When you're out in the woods, it's a lot harder to just run back home for something you forgot. Therefore, a well-packed backpack is the savvy forager's best friend! In this section, we're going to go over what the ideal forager's backpack looks like, with a brief explanation of each of its features and contents. You don't need to run out and spend hundreds of dollars on your foraging gear—most of this will be things you already have or can acquire quite easily!

Note—use common sense when coming up with your backpack! You'll need to check off this whole list if you're going deep into the wilderness, but if you're just grabbing a basket and heading five minutes into the trees down the road, you don't need such an extensive kit.

- **Proper attire**: comfortable clothing, long, loose-fitting pants, high socks, and well-fitting hiking boots.
    - Your pants should be tucked into the high socks before you put your boots on. Not only will long pants, the extra layer of fabric from socks, and boots give you a little "armor" in case of an unexpected snake encounter, but they will also help keep you safe from ticks if you're walking through plants, grass, and brush.
    - Proper boots will ensure you can traverse the terrain without twisting an ankle or otherwise injuring yourself—make sure they're snugly laced to stop them from slipping and sliding around.
- **Hat, sunscreen, and sunglasses**
    - You don't need to put yourself at risk of a sunburn (and worsen your long-term skin health) in search of mushrooms.
    - Having shade for your eyes protects them from strain and helps you keep a better eye out for mushrooms!
- **Bug spray**

- o The Pacific Northwest is humid in many regions, and mosquitoes may be out in force. Enough said!

- **Bear spray, pepper spray, or Mace**
    - o Not just for bears! In the very unlikely event of an attack by a bear, wolf, cougar, or other large animal, this could save your life.
    - o Be sure you know how to use your spray, including its range, how to remove the safety lock, and which direction the solution comes out!

- **Extra warm layer**
    - o When heading out to the wilderness, aim to dress in layers—for example, if it's a chilly day, wear a long-sleeved shirt, a sweater, and a lighter jacket instead of a T shirt and a heavy coat. This will let you adjust how warmly you're dressed as needed.
    - o Bring or wear one more layer than you think you'll need. Especially during autumn, some of the PNW can have very unpredictable weather. Worst case scenario—what if you get lost, and you're still outside when the temperature falls at night?

- **Baskets, pouches, bags, or containers for harvest**
    - o Leather and canvas pouches, paper bags, and even woven baskets with or without lids are popular options.

- o Searching Amazon for mushroom foraging gear will turn up many handy pouch options that clip onto your belt or backpack.
- **Gloves**
  - o Select tough gardening gloves that cover your wrists and are resistant to thorns and cuts.
  - o This will prevent a nasty cut if your knife slips, stop thorns, brambles, and sharp twigs from scratching you, and hopefully provide a layer of protection in the event of a snake bite!
- **Pocket knife**
  - o Choose a sharp knife that folds or comes with a cover, and cover the blade when not in use.
- **Snacks**
  - o Foraging uses up a lot of energy, so bring along nutrient-dense, high-calorie snacks like trail mix, nuts, dried fruit, or protein bars for a boost.
  - o You could even work a picnic into your plan.
- **Plenty of water in non-breakable bottle**
  - o Choose a durable bottle you trust—if you can't throw it on the ground without it breaking, it's not the bottle you're looking for. What if it broke when you were six hours deep in the woods, or if you were lost?

- o Nalgene bottles, although made of plastic, are lightweight, practically unbreakable, come with a handy loop for carrying or attaching it to your backpack, and can easily be acquired online for less than $15.
- **Water purification tablets**
  - o This is the first in the "just in case" entries on our list. If you get lost, you're in a better position if you can refill your water.
  - o Don't drink non-purified river or stream water unless it's a dire survival situation.
  - o You can also purchase water bottles with filters attached, but these usually still require purification.
- **First aid kit**
  - o Be realistic with this, to avoid taking up unnecessary space. If you get hurt in the woods, patching yourself up long enough to get home or to medical care is the priority. Therefore, a small, basic first aid kit will suffice.
  - o Try to ensure there are at least a couple copies of each item, in case you have multiple injuries, or more than one person is injured.
  - o Don't forget an up-to-date first aid manual with clear images or diagrams! If you can't see it when your hands are shaking, find a clearer one.

- Search for a "Type 1 (Personal) First Aid Kit" online for ample articles about what a basic first aid kit looks like—or simply buy one online!
- **Survival blanket**
  - This is just in case the worst happens, and you find yourself lost. They can also be placed on a person who is going into shock to help them keep warm.
  - A survival blanket is a lightweight blanket made of synthetic materials such as *metalized polyethylene* that will reflect as much body heat as possible back to you.
  - These can fold up quite small, and are included in some first aid kits—if yours doesn't have one, you should get one and add it yourself!
- **Flashlight, flares, and whistle**
  - These are all things you won't necessarily need if you're not going far, but if you're going deep in the wilderness, you should have them in case you lose your way.
  - Flares and a whistle will help you signal distress if you're lost, or injured and can't get out of the woods.
  - A flashlight can help you signal as well, but will also prevent you from being stuck in the dark if you're still outside when the sun sets.

Foraging Ethically

As foraging becomes more and more popular, there's been more and more of a discussion about how to do it ethically. There are a few things to consider making sure you don't run afoul of the law, or accidentally do damage to the environment.

Respect private property: No exceptions! When you go foraging, you need to know exactly where you are and if you're allowed to be there. Wandering onto private property is a great way to get a trespassing citation or worse. Therefore, only forage on private property if you know the owner and have permission to be there.

Watch your step. As we said in the first section—you're not the only one in the woods! Watching where you step can help you *also* avoid stepping needlessly on plants, fungi, and other forms of life like reptiles and insects. It will also keep you safe from tripping—and snakes!

Think carefully about what you're picking. Several ethical foraging guidelines can be summed up with this statement!

- A lot of our identification instructions in Section 2 involve picking and cutting open an individual specimen, to check for bruise color, the color of the inner flesh, gills hidden under a veil, or other identifying traits you can't see on the outside. This is necessary for your own safety, but choose specimens that are in good condition for this purpose to make sure you can actually discern the traits you're checking for and reduce how many you have to discard.

- Spend a little time looking around the surrounding area before you start harvesting. Ecosystems are surprisingly delicate, and rely on the presence of certain species to function. Removing the last of a species for a localized area can have a domino effect that harms much more than just the mushroom you took.
- For the same reason, don't completely strip a patch or cluster of mushrooms! Leave at least five fruiting bodies behind for each you harvest.
- A lot of mushrooms go further than you might think. Avoid taking more than you need.

Leave only footprints behind. There's a common saying among hikers and other wilderness lovers: "Take only pictures, leave only footprints." While the entire point of foraging is to take home more than pictures, leaving only footprints is sound advice. Don't litter, and *especially* don't leave anything edible behind—you don't want something like a bear to find it and learn that a lot of humans carry food!

Avoid destroying the mycelium. As we explained in Section 2, the mycelium is an expansive network of underground fibrils that joins individual fruiting bodies together, sometimes over a vast area. If you avoid damaging the mycelium, you also help yourself—the same species will sprout another flush the next time conditions are right, so you can come back again and again! To protect the mycelium, carefully cut mushrooms at the base with a sharp knife, or pinch at the base and twist the fruiting body *off*, instead of yanking *out*. Don't unnecessarily dig in the ground around places you see mushrooms.

Tip: Chicken of the woods and similar polypores have a tough, younger outer layer that can be cut off, leaving the rest of the mushroom still attached.

Preparing, Preserving, and Cooking Foraged Mushrooms

Once you get your mushrooms home, the fun isn't over! Now it's time to put some healthy foraged food on the table for you and your family. In this section, we'll go over some ideas for how to prepare your mushrooms for consumption, and *also* give three recipes you can use as inspiration for how to cook with your wild mushroom harvest!

Getting Mushrooms Ready For Cooking or Preservation

All wild mushrooms need to be thoroughly cooked before consumption—*no* exceptions, not even mushrooms like chanterelles or king boletes/porcinis that can be found in stores. Cooking kills off some kinds of bacteria you won't find lurking in the produce section of the supermarket. This is why (some) store-bought mushrooms can be eaten raw while foraged mushrooms can't, even if they're the same species!

There's a common assumption that you shouldn't wash your mushrooms because you'll "wash away the flavor" but this advice is outdated. The mushrooms have been growing outside for days or weeks before you got your hands on them, and have almost been rained on several times. A bit of water from the kitchen sink won't be a problem! However, there is a kernel of truth—you don't want to absolutely drench your mushrooms, as many of them are very absorbent and can become soggy.

Start cleaning a few hours before you cook. This will give the mushrooms time to air dry before you toss them in a pan, which gives them a better texture and bite. As you clean, **double check each *individual* fruiting body's identity**—a sneaky death cap getting mixed with common puffballs, for example, could result in an *entirely* preventable tragedy.

Next, cut off whatever you can't eat. There's probably a hard, dirty tip at the end of the stem, "scars" and other hardened spots, damaged, bruised areas, and so on. Using a *sharp* knife or even a potato peeler, cut the hard inedible bits off. Some mushrooms are only edible in one part of the fruiting body or only in the younger flesh, so if this is the case, remove whatever isn't edible now. For example, the slime of the slimy spike cap isn't edible, so remove the outer layer of these mushrooms before proceeding.

The next step is to start running the kitchen sink at a lukewarm temperature. Using a small brush (any clean soft-bristled toothbrush will do), gently scrub the mushroom all over to remove dirt and debris, holding it under the water for *brief* periods. Pat the mushrooms dry with a clean paper towel—but you won't get them fully dry since water has been absorbed by the mushroom. Take a sharp knife and slice each fruiting body in half. Do you see holes on the inside of the flesh—or even visible bugs? This is a sign of a parasite infestation. In some larger species with firm flesh, you're fine to just cut off the infested part if it's localized to one area, but in smaller species, assume the whole thing is inedible. As the common saying about food safety goes: *when in doubt, throw it out!*

The last step is to lay the mushrooms out on clean, dry paper towels to air-dry for a few hours while you prepare the rest of your ingredients!

So how can you cook or prepare your mushrooms to make sure all the work you've put in was worth it? You've already seen a ton of ideas in the *uses* section of the mushroom profiles in the last section, but we've included some more here!

Preserving Wild Mushrooms

People have been preserving mushrooms for thousands of years, by different methods. We've briefly described a few here for your consideration.

Refrigeration: Typically, mushrooms last 3-5 days in the fridge. The proper way to store them is in a paper bag—this prevents them from getting soggy with the condensation that would collect in a plastic wrap or bag, or in a plastic, metal, or glass container.

Canning: Canned foods can last for months to years if the canning process was done properly and if the seal isn't interrupted. Depending on the recipe, canning can be done in a *water bath* which is essentially a big stockpot of boiling water, or a *pressure canner*, which looks similar but comes with a lid that forms a seal and uses pressurized steam to reach higher temperatures.

Freeze-drying: This is how MREs, or meals ready to eat, are made! MREs are packaged meals distributed to service-people in the military when they head out in the field, and won't necessarily be able to access fresh food. Freeze-drying maintains most of the nutritional value of the food, and does better at preserving texture and taste than some other preservation methods while also making food last for years or decades. Just add water, and it's ready to eat! Freeze-dried mushrooms can last 20 years in some cases. Freeze-drying involves a piece of special equipment called, as you might expect, a freeze-dryer!

Drying/dehydration: This is by *far* the most popular way to preserve mushrooms, and requires no special equipment at all. Drying essentially involves putting thin-sliced mushrooms in the over at lower heat for a few hours, which causes around 20% of the moisture to evaporate. Dried mushrooms can be stored for months to years in a sealed container, and whenever you're ready to cook them, you simply soak them in water to reconstitute them back to their previous form!

Drying Mushrooms

Since drying in an oven or dehydrator is by far the most popular—and possibly just the best—way to preserve mushrooms, we've included some notes about how to do it here.

A dehydrator is essentially a mini-oven designed for drying food. These are convenient if you forage a lot, because drying in the oven naturally makes it so you can't use the oven for that period of time. However, unless you're drying mushrooms often, buying a dehydrator isn't really something you need to worry about—the oven is perfectly capable! For the rest of this section, we'll assume you're using an oven, but with a dehydrator the principle is the same.

Preheat the oven on its lowest setting—if this is above 150 degrees Fahrenheit, leave the door ajar to let more air circulate. Slice the mushrooms thinly, aiming for 0.2 inches thick. It's important that the mushrooms are *evenly* sliced, or else you'll have a thicker piece that doesn't fully dry, starts to rot in storage, and ruins the entire batch! There are tools with evenly-spaced blades on the market for this, or simply use a sharp paring knife and a careful hand!

When the mushrooms are dry and sliced up, lay them out on a baking sheet lined with parchment paper, ensuring there are no overlaps—in fact, they shouldn't even touch! Give them a last minute pat with a paper towel to remove any extra moisture, and toss them in the oven for an hour or so. Each 30 minutes, pull them out and pat dry again to remove any moisture they've released.

When you think your mushrooms are ready, let them cool and check them by trying to fold them in half. They should crack when you try to bend them, and produce a sound when they do! If they're not ready, turn them over and put them back in for another 30 minutes and repeat the process.

So What Can I Actually Do With Mushrooms?

We've talked a lot about cooking with mushrooms in this book, but now we're getting down to the specifics. In this section, we're going to go over common dishes and other uses for foraged mushrooms to give you some inspiration for how to use your first harvest! Need more ideas? Check out the original recipes below!

Virtually every world cuisine incorporates mushrooms, each in a unique way. Mushrooms are a common component in many Asian cuisines, as well as in fusion and Asian-inspired dishes throughout the world! Not only are endless mushroom species found in Asia, but the unique savory flavor is also an excellent example of *umami*, a highly sought-after flavor profile in Japanese cuisine.

In Japanese cuisine, mushrooms are sometimes sliced small and added to sushi or related dishes as well—for example, the large futomaki roll usually contains (among other fresh and cooked ingredients) shiitake mushrooms, which have a rich flavor many foraged mushrooms could stand in for if you wanted to try making these extra-thick sushi rolls at home!

A major use of mushrooms in Chinese cuisine is in *dim sum*–a style of meal originating from the Cantonese region. Traditionally, dim sum refers to a meal of small plates, including dumplings, for breakfast or brunch. In dim sum, mushrooms can be stuffed and served as a plate of their own or mixed into dumplings with meat and/or vegetables. Some mushrooms with a unique look or flavor are added to special dishes—across China and neighboring countries, jelly ear mushrooms are selected as a traditional ingredient in hot and sour soup.

Sautéing is a big part of cooking with mushrooms throughout the world, as it doesn't destroy the mushroom's excellent texture. French cuisine, for example, includes dishes where mushrooms are sauteed in butter with seasonings such as savory herbs, garlic, salt, pepper, and lemon.

Not to be outdone, Italian cuisine favors sautéing mushrooms in olive oil with its own range of flavors, but also capitalizes on the fact that mushrooms pair well with acidic flavors, like vinegars and tomatoes. Mushrooms can also be sliced thin, sauteed, and then simmered into pasta sauces, or sliced up and added to lasagna, dumplings, and other dishes where food is stuffed inside pasta.

These are just some of the most common examples of mushrooms being used in cuisine that we thought would demonstrate the range of their usefulness! Here's a few more ideas found across the world:

- Mushroom teas can be a delicious and soothing savory treat!
    - Simply use a knife or food processor to cut mushrooms down into chunks no larger than frozen peas, and mix them with plain black tea leaves, whole spices, dried citrus peels, herbs, and/or dried fruit—don't be afraid to get creative and combine flavors you think work well together!
    - Soak dried mushroom pieces and other ingredients in water just below boiling temperature for approximately five minutes, then strain the liquid into a mug. Serve immediately with milk, honey, or whatever condiments you desire, or let it cool and serve over ice!
- Mushrooms are an excellent addition to hearty soups and stews, since most species' savory flavor pairs well with beef, pork, onions, and garlic.
    - Hint: Use the water you soaked dried mushrooms in to reconstitute them as a mushroom broth!
- Mushrooms stir-fried with an Asian-inspired sauce and your choice of meat and vegetables is a hearty meal–not to mention quick to put together on weeknights!

Some traditional medical practices, including Traditional Chinese Medicine and the traditional practices of various Indigenous peoples in North America, include mushrooms as a regular ingredient in medicines—for example, jelly ears are used in TCM to manage blood sugar problems. Many people incorporate this kind of practice into their health routines because of their cultural beliefs, or because they've had it work before! There's nothing wrong with delving into traditional medicine, and there's even scientific data to back up some uses—but make sure you talk to a licensed physician before

Recipes

Mushroom Omelet

Who doesn't love a Western omelet with mushrooms? This, however, is not that—but a recipe we dreamt up to showcase the rich savory flavors of mushrooms like the king bolete! In this recipe, the mushrooms are sauteed in butter and paired with caramelized onions, herbs, and sundried tomato.

This recipe serves 1, but you can multiply it as many times as you like.

What you need:

- A handful of finely chopped fresh or reconstituted mushrooms, approximately ¼ cup
- 2.5 tablespoons of butter, divided
- Half a small onion, finely chopped

- Sundried tomatoes from a jar—use a fork or chopsticks to pick them out and add as many as you like to the omelet
- 2 large eggs or 3 medium eggs
- Splash of milk
- Approximately 1-2 tsp Italian herb blend, or make your own blend of parsley, rosemary, thyme, and oregano
- A handful of mozzarella cheese, or more if you prefer!
- Salt and pepper to taste (approximately ½ tsp each)

Steps:

- Start by melting 1 tbsp butter in a saucepan over medium heat. When the butter starts to shimmer, gently add the onion. Let cook for 15 minutes, stirring periodically, while you prepare the rest of the recipe.
- Crack the eggs into a large mixing bowl, add the splash of milk, the herb blend, and salt and pepper. Whisk until a smooth mixture is formed.
- At the end of 15 minutes, the onions may not be fully caramelized, but they'll finish over the next step. Add the mushrooms and 0.5 tbsp of butter *if needed*—if the first portion you added is still simmering away, there's no need to add more, but if it's burned up or evaporated, go ahead!
- Sauté onions and mushrooms together for 15 min. Then, use a spatula to spread the contents of the pan out evenly.

- Add the sundried tomatoes and cook 5-7 minutes.
- *Slowly* pour the egg and herb mixture into the pan, giving it time to spread out and cover the rest of the ingredients! Melt more butter if needed.
- When you notice the edges of the egg getting dry and turning up, use a spatula or flipper to *gently* try to get underneath. When the omelet is ready to be turned, sprinkle the cheese all over the surface and fold the omelet in half, trapping the cheese in the middle.
- Flip the folded omelet over, cook 2 minutes, then fold again the other way, remove from heat and serve with a side of bacon or sausage!

Miso Mushroom Noodle Soup

Miso is a form of fermented soybean paste that comes in white and red varieties, which may be added to broths and sauces to flavor them! Miso broth is also a delight to look at, as it takes on a lovely soft opaque white or tan color.

For this recipe, we recommend using delicate mushrooms that dry and reconstitute well, and have a sweet flavor, like fairy ring mushrooms, chanterelles, hedgehogs, or jelly ears! You can even mix them for extra variety.

You'll also notice that there's room for variety in this recipe! Since many of the components are strong-tasting, consider adding them gradually to the broth while tasting. Want to take it up a notch? Use Japanese-style pickled eggs instead of soft-boiled to boost your soup even more!

This recipe serves 4.

What you need:

- 1 package of rice noodles, medium thickness
- 1 large chicken breast, cooked
- ~1 cup of thinly sliced dried mushrooms
- 4 eggs, soft boiled
- 6 cups of broth—chicken, mushroom, vegetable, etc.
- **Miso paste, red or white, to taste (approximately ⅓ cup)**
- 1/4 cup soy sauce
- 2 tbsp honey (divided)
- 1-2 thumbs of minced fresh ginger (divided)
- 2-6 cloves of garlic (divided)
- Salt and pepper to taste

Steps:

- Prepare rice noodles according to package instructions. Drain and set aside.
- Cook the chicken breast according to your preferred method, and let it rest for 10 minutes. Using two forks, shred the chicken into a bowl, and toss with a generous splash of soy sauce, salt and pepper, approximately a half-tbsp of honey, 1-2 cloves of garlic and half a thumb of mixed ginger. Cover and store in the refrigerator while you prepare the next step.
- Start the broth in a large saucepan at a simmer on medium heat on the stove, and add approximately a

tablespoon of miso paste, along with part of the soy sauce, garlic, ginger, and honey. The ingredients will take time to dissolve, especially the miso paste. Stir regularly while you work on the other steps, taste, and add more of anything you think it needs.

- In a second saucepan, boil enough water on medium-high heat to cover all four eggs. Once the water is boiling, gently lower the eggs into the water, and set a timer for 5-6 minutes.

- Retrieve the soft-boiled eggs when the timer goes off, and lower into cold water to cool. After 10 minutes, you can start peeling them, and then cut them in half to expose their yolks.

- In a colander or steamer basket—you want the mushrooms to be submerged but still under control—start simmering the mushrooms in the broth. In 10-15 minutes (assuming they're a delicate species) they should be *al dente*—if not fully reconstituted. When you're happy with them, take them out of the broth and set aside. Season with a little salt and pepper.

- Now, get a large bowl for each person partaking in the meal, and divide the rice noodles into four sections. On top of the rice noodles, add the mushrooms, chicken, egg, and any other condiments you might want—we suggest Mung beans or nori seaweed!

- Carefully pour the broth into each bowl and serve immediately.

Mushroom Pot Pie

Pot pies are a *super* comforting lunch or snack on any cold, wet day, and also a great way to mix carbs, vegetables, and meat into one cozy meal. Pot pies are essentially a pie crust that is used to line a pot, filled with a savory mix of fruit and vegetables, and then baked in the oven.

Don't have that much mushroom, just have smaller ones, or don't feel fed until you have meat? Consider making this mushroom pot pie a mix of your favorite meat *and* mushrooms inside.

This recipe serves 2-3.

What you need:

- 1 medium yellow onion, finely chopped
- 1 9-inch pie crust
- ½ cup butter
- ¼ cup white flour (all purpose)
- **⅓ cup of cream**
- 2 cups of your favorite vegetables—carrots, peas, and corn are common choices! If the vegetables are large, cut them into smaller-than bite sized chunks.
- Optional: add your favorite herbs and spices with the vegetables!
- 2 cups of shredded white foraged mushrooms (e.g., king bolete, giant puffball, oyster), washed and dried
- 1 ¾ cup of broth

- ○ Hint: Use mushroom broth from reconstituting mushrooms if you have it! Otherwise, vegetable stock is fine, or you can match the broth to meat if you're using any.
- Sea salt and black pepper to taste

Steps:

- Follow package directions for preparing pie crust.
- Preheat the oven to 425 degrees Fahrenheit.
- Whisk together flour with a few generous cracks of sea salt and black pepper in a large bowl.
- Add cream and broth to the bowl and whisk until a homogenous mixture is formed.
- In a large saucepan, melt the butter over low-medium heat until you notice the edges start to bubble and brown.
- Add onion and cook until onion is translucent, and you can smell its natural sugars. Stir constantly.
- Still stirring constantly, **slowly** pour the mixture in the bowl into the saucepan.
- Stir at a simmer until the mixture is as even as possible.
- In a new bowl, toss mushroom, spices, herbs, and vegetable pieces until thoroughly mixed.
- Slowly add ingredients to the saucepan while stirring. When the mixture is thick enough that it bubbles and is hard to stir, it's ready.
- Grease a 9 inch pie pan and line with prepared crust.

- Pour the mixture in the saucepan slowly into the crust, using a spatula and wooden spoon to even it out.
- Place the top half of the pie crust on top and seal according to package instructions. Cut slits in the top of the pie so steam can escape.
- Place in oven and bake for 20 minutes.
- Remove from oven and wrap tin foil around outer edges of the pie crust.
- Put the pan back in the oven for 20 minutes.
- Remove the pan from the oven. If the pot pie is golden brown with a crispy outside, it's ready! Let stand 5-10 minutes, and then serve hot with a roll or as a side to meat.

Conclusion

Congratulations on taking your first step to becoming a master mushroom hunter. With knowledge on your side, you're ready to head out and start foraging. Take this guide with you, or if you don't want to carry a whole book, take photos of the pages describing the mushrooms you're looking for! We intended for this book to be a trusty companion for foragers of *any* skill level who understand that in order to be safe, every mushroom identification needs to be 100% positive and 100% accurate!

Final note: If you enjoyed this book, or if you find it useful, kindly consider leaving us a review! Positive reviews bring our book higher in the Amazon listing, helping us share it with more and more aspiring or experienced foragers in the PNW and beyond!

References

Adamant, A. (2018, September 21). *Foraging shaggy mane mushrooms.* Practical Self Reliance. https://practicalselfreliance.com/shaggy-mane-mushrooms/

Bears in Alberta. (2014). *Preventing bear encounters.* In AlbertaParks.ca. https://www.albertaparks.ca/media/123478/bear-smart-brochure-web.pdf

Bergo, A. (2013a, March 18). *The forager's guide to hedgehog mushrooms.* Forager Chef. https://foragerchef.com/hedgehog-mushrooms/

Bergo, A. (2013b, March 27). *Saffron milk caps.* Forager Chef. https://foragerchef.com/painted-on-the-stones-saffron-milk-caps/

Bergo, A. (2015, July 14). *Fairy ring mushrooms / mousserons.* Forager Chef. https://foragerchef.com/fairy-ring-mushrooms-marasmius-oreades/

Bergo, A. (2016, February 19). *Cauliflower mushrooms: The noodle fungus.* Forager Chef. https://foragerchef.com/cauliflower-mushrooms-sparassis/

Bergo, A. (2018, August 25). *Giant hedgehog mushrooms: "Spreaders."* Forager Chef.

https://foragerchef.com/giant-hedgehog-mushrooms-a-k-a-spreaders/

Berman, K. (2000, October 1). *Pairings: Wild and wonderful mushrooms.* Wine Enthusiast. https://www.winemag.com/2000/10/01/pairings-wild-and-wonderful-mushrooms/

Blizzard, T. (2017, April 21). *Responsible and sustainable mushroom picking.* Modern Forager. https://www.modern-forager.com/sustainable-mushroom-picking/

Burke Museum Herbarium. (2021). *Burke herbarium image collection.* Washington.edu. https://biology.burke.washington.edu/herbarium/imagecollection/taxon.php?Taxon=Morchella%20elata

Catanoso, J. (2021, September 1). *Old-growth forests of Pacific northwest could be key to climate action.* Mongabay Environmental News. https://news.mongabay.com/2021/09/old-growth-forests-of-pacific-northwest-could-be-key-to-climate-action/

Codekas, C. (2016, August 21). *Foraging for oyster mushrooms.* Grow Forage Cook Ferment. https://www.growforagecookferment.com/foraging-oyster-mushrooms/

Comb tooth fungus identification: Pictures, habitat, season & spore print. Hericium coralloides. (2021). Edible Wild Food. https://www.ediblewildfood.com/comb-tooth-fungus.aspx

Common puffball. (2022). Kitsap Peninsula Mycological Society. https://kitsapmushrooms.org/edible-mushrooms/common-puffball/

Cougar. (2022). Washington Department of Fish & Wildlife. https://wdfw.wa.gov/species-habitats/species/puma-concolor#conflict

Dangerous wildlife. (2022). Washington Department of Fish & Wildlife. **https://wdfw.wa.gov/species-habitats/living/dangerous-wildlife**

The edible and medicinal wood ear mushroom: Auricularia auricula. Foraging, identifying and preparing this wild mushroom. (2017, March 3). The Foraged Foodie. https://foragedfoodie.blogspot.com/2017/03/foraging-edible-medicinal-wood-ear-mushroom.html

Emergency Essentials. (2014). *Surviving a wolf attack.* Be Prepared. https://beprepared.com/blogs/articles/surviving-a-wolf-attack

Emese, & Nandi. (2021, November 3). *Guide to cooking with wood ear mushrooms (10 must-try recipes).* My Pure Plants. https://mypureplants.com/wood-ear-mushrooms/

Giant puffball identification: Pictures, habitat, season & spore print. Calvatia gigantea (2021). Edible Wild Food. https://www.ediblewildfood.com/giant-puffball.aspx

Gobush, K. S. (2021). *Pacific northwest forests: Sustaining wildlife, people and the planet.* Defenders of Wildlife.

https://defenders.org/blog/2021/03/pacific-
northwest-forests-sustaining-wildlife-people-and-
planet

Harris, H. (2017, April 18). *Things to take with you when you go foraging.* The Homesteading Hippy. https://thehomesteadinghippy.com/foraging-for-wild-edibles/

Horse mushroom (2022). iNaturalist. http://inaturalist.org/guide_taxa/1185238

Julson, E. (2018). *9 Health Benefits of Lion's Mane Mushroom (Plus Side Effects).* Healthline. https://www.healthline.com/nutrition/lions-mane-mushroom

Kuo, M. (2020). *Hydnum repandum.* Mushroom Expert. https://www.mushroomexpert.com/hydnum_repa ndum.html

Kuo, M. (2021). *Guepinia helvelloides.* Mushroom Expert. https://www.mushroomexpert.com/guepinia_helv elloides.html

Lactarius deliciosus. (2018). Mushrooms Up! Edible and Poisonous Species of Coastal BC and the Pacific Northwest. https://www.zoology.ubc.ca/~biodiv/mushroom/ L_deliciosus.html

Meredith, L. (2019). *How to dry mushrooms in your oven.* The Spruce Eats. https://www.thespruceeats.com/how-to-dry-mushrooms-oven-method-1327547

Morris, R. (2017, January 30). *Magical mushroom pairings.* Wine Enthusiast. https://www.winemag.com/2017/01/30/magical-mushroom-pairings/

Mountain lion safety. (2021, October 19). U.S. Fish & Wildlife Service. https://www.fws.gov/story/mountain-lion-safety

Niemiec, S., Ahrens, G., Willits, S., & Hibbs, D. (1995). *Hardwoods of the Pacific northwest.* https://hsc.forestry.oregonstate.edu/sites/hsc/files/Hardwoods%20of%20the%20Pacific%20Northwest.pdf

Foraging in the Pacific northwest and Canada. (2019). Northern Bushcraft. https://northernbushcraft.com/

O'Reilly, P. (2016a). *Gomphidius glutinosus, slimy spike mushroom.* First Nature. https://www.first-nature.com/fungi/gomphidius-glutinosus.php

O'Reilly, P. (2016b). *Marasmius oreades, fairy ring champignon mushroom.* First Nature. https://www.first-nature.com/fungi/marasmius-oreades.php

O'Reilly, P. (2016c). *Russula claroflava, yellow swamp brittlegill mushroom.* First Nature. https://www.first-nature.com/fungi/russula-claroflava.php

O'Reilly, P. (2016d). *Xerocomellus chrysenteron, red-cracking bolete mushroom.* First Nature. https://www.first-nature.com/fungi/xerocomellus-chrysenteron.php

Owerko, C. (2020, October 28). *Foraging in the Pacific northwest.* Silvercore Advanced Training Systems. https://silvercore.ca/2020/10/28/foraging-in-the-pacific-northwest/

Pacific northwest websites for wildlife. (2022). Go Northwest! A Travel Guide. https://www.gonorthwest.com/Visitor/webs/wildlife.htm

King bolete mushrooms. (2014, July 30). Pacific Northwest Wild Mushrooms. https://pnwwildmushrooms.com/wild-mushrooms/king-bolete-mushrooms

Parker, B. (2021, October 18). *Hedgehog mushroom recipes – how to use them?* Mushroom Site. https://mushroomsite.com/2021/10/18/hedgehog-mushroom-recipes/

Perez, L. (2020, December 10). *Pacific northwest wetlands.* ArcGIS StoryMaps. https://storymaps.arcgis.com/stories/5cd257024b9a4b60bd261f02a0792eb2

Puffball mushroom, you'll be ok if you follow one ID feature. Eat the Planet. https://eattheplanet.org/puffball-mushroom-youll-be-ok-if-you-follow-one-id-feature/

Morel mushrooms. (2014, July 31). Pacific Northwest Wild Mushrooms. https://pnwwildmushrooms.com/wild-mushrooms/morel-mushrooms

REI Staff. (2019, July 31). *Hiking checklist: What to bring on a hike*. REI; REI. https://www.rei.com/learn/expert-advice/day-hiking-checklist.html

Schreiber, L. M. (2007, June 6). *There's something about morels*. Wine Enthusiast. https://www.winemag.com/2007/06/06/theres-something-about-morels/

Seersholm, F. V., Werndly, D. J., Grealy, A., Johnson, T., Keenan Early, E. M., Lundelius, E. L., Winsborough, B., Farr, G. E., Toomey, R., Hansen, A. J., Shapiro, B., Waters, M. R., McDonald, G., Linderholm, A., Stafford, T. W., & Bunce, M. (2020). Rapid range shifts and megafaunal extinctions associated with late Pleistocene climate change. *Nature Communications,* 11(1). https://doi.org/10.1038/s41467-020-16502-3

Shaw, H. (2012, November 29). *Agaricus campestris - identifying and cooking meadow mushrooms*. Hunter Angler Gardener Cook. https://honest-food.net/meadow-mushroom-recipe-escoffier/

Species fact sheets. (2022). Washington Department of Fish & Wildlife. https://wdfw.wa.gov/species-habitats/living/species-facts

Spector, D. (2012, June 29). *What to do if you are attacked by a pack of wolves*. Business Insider. https://www.businessinsider.com/what-to-do-if-you-are-attacked-by-a-pack-of-wolves-2012-6

Spryut, J. (2021). *Western rattlesnake*. The Canadian Encyclopedia.

https://www.thecanadianencyclopedia.ca/en/articl
e/western-rattlesnake

How to identify and pick porcini / king bolete / cep. (2015,
September 24). The Greedy Vegan.
https://thegreedyvegan.com/how-to-identify-and-
pick-porcini/

Tjandra, C. (2019, September 23). *Giant puffball mushroom, a
soft and tasty delicacy.* Eat the Planet.
https://eattheplanet.org/giant-puffball-mushroom-
a-soft-and-tasty-delicacy

Tkaczyk, F. (2022). *Edible wild mushrooms.* Alderleaf
Wilderness College.
https://www.wildernesscollege.com/edible-wild-
mushrooms.html

Vancouver Island Mushrooms. (2022). *Oyster mushroom guide.*
West Coast Forager.
https://www.westcoastforager.com/wild-edible-
mushrooms/oyster-mushroom-guide

Waring, R. H., & Franklin, J. F. (1979). *Evergreen coniferous
forests of the Pacific northwest.* Science, 204(4400),
1380–1386.
https://doi.org/10.1126/science.204.4400.1380

Watson, M. (2021). *What are oyster mushrooms?* The Spruce
Eats. https://www.thespruceeats.com/what-are-
oyster-mushrooms-4172003

Williams, M. (2012). *Horse mushrooms – edibility, identification,
distribution.* Galloway Wild Foods.

https://gallowaywildfoods.com/july-horse-mushrooms/

Instructions for how to clean mushrooms. (2022). Wine Forest Wild Foods. https://wineforest.com/pages/how-to-clean-mushrooms

Wolf safety. (2022). BCParks.ca; Province of British Columbia. https://bcparks.ca/explore/misc/wolves/

Young, B. (2017, July 26). *Rattlesnake bite.* Healthline; Healthline Media. https://www.healthline.com/health/rattlesnake-bite

Image References

Pixabay. (2013). *Image by DomenicBlair from Pixabay.* Pixabay. https://pixabay.com/photos/giant-puffballs-calvatia-gigantea-185481/

Pixabay. (2014a). *Image by Aniko Boros from Pixabay.* Pixabay. https://pixabay.com/photos/oyster-mushrooms-wood-autumn-360747/

Pixabay. (2020b). *Image by Hans Linde from Pixabay.* https://pixabay.com/photos/mushrooms-schopf-comatus-shaggy-mane-5665580/

Pixabay. (2014b). *Image by Jan Mallander from Pixabay.* Pixabay.

https://pixabay.com/photos/cauliflower-mushroom-mushroom-edible-562982/

Pixabay. (2014). *Image by Gaby Stein from Pixabay.* Pixabay. https://pixabay.com/nl/photos/russula-paddestoelen-woud-val-253257/

Pixabay. (2016). *Image by Janet Herman from Pixabay.* Pixabay. https://pixabay.com/nl/photos/paardenpaddestoel-agaricus-arvensis-1254040/

Pixabay. (2016a). *Image by Janet Herman from Pixabay.* Pixabay. https://pixabay.com/photos/horse-mushroom-agaricus-arvensis-1254040/

Pixabay. (2016b). *Image by Kerstin Herrmann from Pixabay.* Pixabay. https://pixabay.com/photos/mushroom-spongy-cauliflower-mushroom-1784177/

Pixabay. (2016c). *Image by Pexels from Pixabay.* Pixabay. https://pixabay.com/photos/mushroom-porcini-king-bolete-1281733/

Pixabay. (2017). *Image by Romdahl from Pixabay.* Pixabay. https://pixabay.com/nl/photos/paddenstoel-trechter-cantharellen-2810447/

Pixabay. (2017a). *Image by adege from Pixabay.* Pixabay. https://pixabay.com/photos/mica-ink-cap-mushrooms-mushroom-fall-2198098/

Pixabay. (2017b). *Image by kellyclampitt from Pixabay.* Pixabay. https://pixabay.com/photos/fungi-chicken-of-the-woods-mushroom-2069479/

Pixabay. (2017c). *Image by kevinsub from Pixabay.* Pixabay. https://pixabay.com/photos/king-bolete-mushroom-green-king-2050796/

Pixabay. (2018a). *Image by adege from Pixabay.* Pixabay. https://pixabay.com/photos/mushrooms-saffron-milk-caps-moss-3700922/

Pixabay. (2018b). *Image by Ulrike Leone from Pixabay.* Pixabay. https://pixabay.com/photos/mushroom-meadow-mushroom-slats-3769313/

Pixabay. (2019a). *Image by Aad Kleijweg from Pixabay.* Pixabay. https://pixabay.com/photos/fungi-forrest-nature-decorative-4501878/

Pixabay. (2019b). *Image by Kevin Cannings from Pixabay.* Pixabay. https://pixabay.com/photos/judas-ear-jews-ear-wood-ear-fungus-4727784/

Pixabay. (2019c). *Image by Kevin Cannings from Pixabay.* Pixabay. https://pixabay.com/photos/judas-ear-jews-ear-wood-ear-fungus-4727778/

Pixabay. (2020a). *Image by dendoktoor from Pixabay.* Pixabay. https://pixabay.com/photos/mushroom-toadstool-forest-inky-cap-5677963/

Pixabay. (2020b). *Image by Sabine Zierer from Pixabay.* Pixabay. https://pixabay.com/photos/mushrooms-toadstools-5712159/

Pixabay. (2021). *Image by adege from Pixabay.* Pixabay. https://pixabay.com/photos/macroperspective-mushroom-moss-6563325/

Pixabay. (2021). *Image by Michael Reichelt from Pixabay.* Pixabay.

https://pixabay.com/photos/mushroom-chanterelle-edible-6598423/

Unsplash. (2020a). *Photo by Beth Macdonald on Unsplash.* Unsplash.com. https://unsplash.com/photos/xHwRfau81rE

Unsplash. (2020b). *Photo by Clyde Gravenberch on Unsplash.* Unsplash.com. https://unsplash.com/photos/uj253l7xPFU

Unsplash. (2021a). Photo by Jan Dommerholt on *Unsplash.* Unsplash.com. https://unsplash.com/photos/ot9mNcH7B9k

Unsplash. (2021a). *Photo by Timothy Dykes on Unsplash.* Unsplash.com. https://unsplash.com/photos/pwE2OExLYc0

Unsplash. (2021b). *Photo by Volodymyr Tokar on Unsplash.* Unsplash.com. https://unsplash.com/photos/XO483Y8_VSQ

Freepik https://www.freepik.com/free-photo/closeup-true-morel-mushrooms-surrounded-by-autumn-leaves-against-blurry-background_20605434.htm

Freepik, https://www.freepik.com/free-photo/two-xerocomellus-chrysenteron-red-cracking bolete_8409145.htm#query=Red%20Cracked%20Bolete&position=0&from_view=search

Pexels, https://www.pexels.com/photo/brown-mushroom-16706/

Rawpixel www.rawpixel.com/image/6055573

Rawpixel, www.rawpixel.com/image/4024045/hericium-coralloides

Istock Photo(2019) photo by Igor Kramar https://www.istockphoto.com/photo/young-edible-mushroom-gomphidius-glutinosus-in-the-spruce-foest-commonly-known-as-gm1130098998-298777541?phrase=Slimy%20Spike%20Cap

Istock Photo(2016) photo by Dabiola https://www.istockphoto.com/nl/foto/hydnum-gm625896602-110328881?phrase=Hedgehog+Mushroom

Istock Photo(2007) photo by Dulezidar https://www.istockphoto.com/nl/foto/mushroom-gm93485472-4338700?phrase=Apricot+Jelly+Mushroom

Istock Photo(2016) photo by Ayakochun https://www.istockphoto.com/nl/foto/lions-mane-mushroom-on-black-background-gm620719564-108305311

www.ingramcontent.com/pod-product-compliance
Lightning Source LLC
LaVergne TN
LVHW042116190726
843493LV00006B/1498